DEAL OR NO DEAL

CAN YOU BEAT THE BANKER ?

EBURY
PRESS

www.dealornodeal.com

First published in Great Britain by Ebury Publishing in 2006

1 3 5 7 9 10 8 6 4 2

Text © Endemol UK 2006

Endemol UK has asserted its right to be identified as the author of this work
under the Copyright, Designs and Patents Act 1988.

Ebury Publishing
Random House, 20 Vauxhall Bridge Road, London SW1V 2SA

Random House Australia (Pty) Limited
20 Alfred Street, Milsons Point, Sydney, New South Wales 2061, Australia

Random House New Zealand Limited
18 Poland Road, Glenfield, Auckland 10, New Zealand

Random House South Africa (Pty) Limited
Isle of Houghton, Corner Boundary Road & Carse O'Gowrie,
Houghton , 2198, South Africa

Random House Publishers India Private Limited
301 World Trade Tower, Hotel Intercontinental Grand Complex,
Barakhamba Lane, New Delhi 110 001, India

The Random House Group Limited Reg. No. 954009
www.randomhouse.co.uk

A CIP catalogue record for this book is available from the British Library.

Designer: info@design-jam.co.uk

Special thanks to:
Glenn Hugill, Series Producer
Richard Hague, Executive Producer
Stephen Boodhun, Producer
Richard Jones, Simon Orr and Joseph Piercy
and the rest of the Deal or No Deal Production team

...and for their help in facilitating this book:
Sian Piddington, Account Manager Consumer Products at Endemol UK
Seema Khan, Head of Consumer Products at Endemol UK

Final thanks to, Uncle Post Production

ISBN: 0091914221
ISBN-13 [from January 2007] : 9780091914226

Papers used by Ebury Press are natural, recyclable products
made from wood grown in sustainable forests.

Printed and bound by Bookmarque, Croydon, Surrey

www.dealornodeal.com

CONTENTS

BANKER'S
INTRODUCTION

H ello. Are you sitting comfortably? I do hope not. As you know, I am a man who likes his fun. A yachting trip to Hawaii, a bottle of claret in San Tropez... but best of all I like to toy with the little people. Little people like you.

So I'm inviting you now to join me on a trip. Not to my beach house in the Maldives you understand, it's just been cleaned. No, I want you to join me now on a journey through the pages of this book.

Delightfully, of course, you won't take any real money away with you but you may learn a few very important things. How to read the run of a game. How to read those magic boxes with my money inside. Maybe, just maybe, how to read me, The Banker.

There is nothing fictional about the trial of wits you have chosen to put yourself through here. All the games in this book actually happened. To real people, with real hopes, real fears and real ambitions... I remember them all... each and every one... like children they are to me...

Such joy as they took that Walk of Wealth; so very desperate to take my money so they might enjoy a spectacular family holiday, or visit a long lost relative or even to finally get the house they'd always dreamed of... only to go home, crushed, with barely enough pennies for the bus fare. Absolutely tragic. And utterly hilarious.

Ah, but then... there's those... those... others. Players who left the game with suitcases stuffed with my hard cash. I'll bet they think they're oh so very clever. 'Look at me', 'I had a system', 'I read the game', 'and I beat the Banker'. Wrong. They got lucky.

Although, there were a couple of exceptions where... you could say... I was thoroughly bested. But I'd rather not talk of those dark days. I'll just pop my private thoughts in my secret diary at bedtime after my nice hot cocoa. Perhaps I'll have a little cry. My mother always said it's good to let the boo-hoos out.

Er... anyway, enough of all that. This is about you, and just how good you think you are. So how are we going to play? We'll start you off with some simple warm ups: spotting my first offer after round 1. Then, when you've toned up those mental biceps, you'll have to tackle a real game. And remember, these were real games, with very real money at stake. My money....

After this, perhaps you'll be ready for the final challenge. You'll know something about how fabulously clever I am. How supremely tough I am. And how devastatingly handsome I am. And you will desire so very much to beat me...

The last test is you and me, head to head. Some of the reds have gone. Some of the blues have gone. I make an offer. At this crucial point, based on all that you have learned, you must face the ultimate question... Deal or No Deal?

Goodbye. I wish you the best of luck and, thank you very much for buying this book. Particularly since I get the profits.

Respectfully yours

The Banker

CHAPTER 01
OPENING OFFERS

R eady? Good. Get comfortable, relax, and let me introduce you to the greatest game of the century, Deal or No Deal. It may seem easy to play at first glance, but there is more to it than you might think. And The Banker is very, very cunning. But he can be beaten, if you stay cool and hold your nerve. I can't help, but I can give you some tips, then it's up to you.

Right. The games you are about to play are all real, so let's get in the mood. Imagine you are sitting at the table with the Banker's telephone on it. The board is in front of you, one side red, one blue. In this first chapter you have to decide what The Banker's opening offer was, based on what is showing on the board in each question. We'll give you three alternatives, just circle the one you think is correct. It starts very easily, but gets harder as you progress through the round.

Remember, when the big numbers go, The Banker's offer will be lower. When the low numbers go early, it'll be higher. You'll get more skilful as you go on, and you'll need to, because every chapter is different and develops your playing ability so that by the final chapter you'll be ready to take on The Banker head to head!

To make things more interesting, you'll be asked to play some games against the clock, as well as The Banker, so make sure you have a pen and a watch handy. At the end of the chapter, fill in your answers on the grid and then check to see how you did. And then see what The Banker thought of your performance! So, let's go. Clear your head, prepare your mind. The phone is ringing...

QUESTION 01
OPENING OFFERS

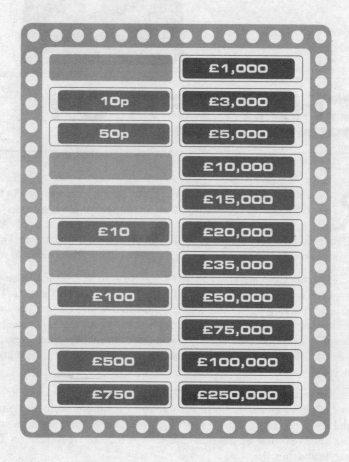

	£1,000
10p	£3,000
50p	£5,000
	£10,000
	£15,000
£10	£20,000
	£35,000
£100	£50,000
	£75,000
£500	£100,000
£750	£250,000

What do you think The Banker's offer was?

A. £4,300   **B.** £52,800   **C.** £11,000

QUESTION 02
OPENING OFFERS

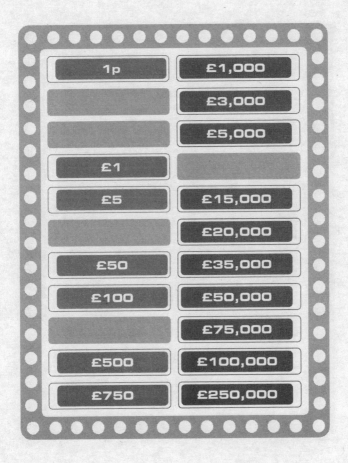

1p	£1,000
	£3,000
	£5,000
£1	
£5	£15,000
	£20,000
£50	£35,000
£100	£50,000
	£75,000
£500	£100,000
£750	£250,000

What do you think The Banker's offer was?

A. £95,000 **B.** £50 **C.** £3,100

QUESTION 03
OPENING OFFERS

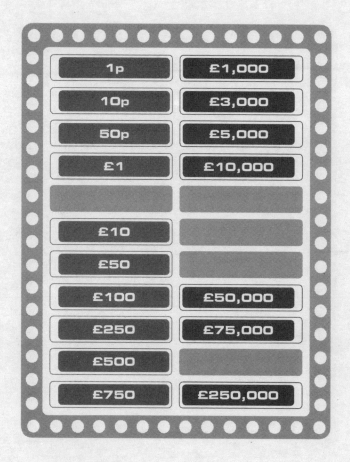

1p	£1,000
10p	£3,000
50p	£5,000
£1	£10,000
£10	
£50	
£100	£50,000
£250	£75,000
£500	
£750	£250,000

What do you think The Banker's offer was?

A. £1,100   **B.** £8,000   **C.** £70,000

QUESTION 04
OPENING OFFERS

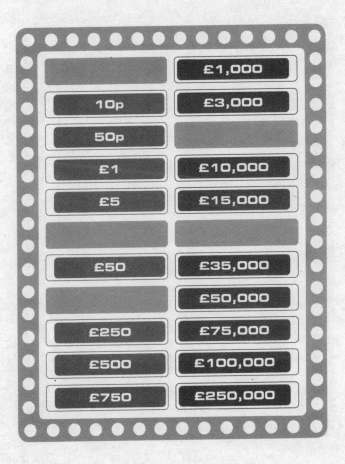

	£1,000
10p	£3,000
50p	
£1	£10,000
£5	£15,000
£50	£35,000
	£50,000
£250	£75,000
£500	£100,000
£750	£250,000

What do you think The Banker's offer was?

A. £8,700 **B.** £6,300 **C.** £12,000

QUESTION 05
OPENING OFFERS

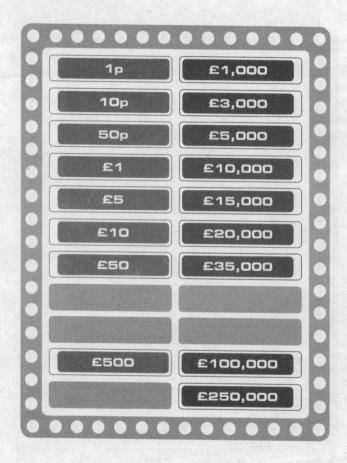

1p	£1,000
10p	£3,000
50p	£5,000
£1	£10,000
£5	£15,000
£10	£20,000
£50	£35,000
£500	£100,000
	£250,000

What do you think The Banker's offer was?

A. £800   **B.** £200   **C.** £100

QUESTION 06
OPENING OFFERS

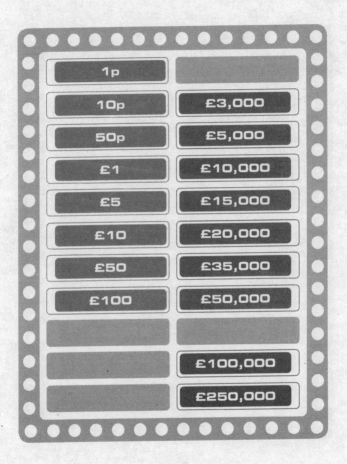

1p	
10p	£3,000
50p	£5,000
£1	£10,000
£5	£15,000
£10	£20,000
£50	£35,000
£100	£50,000
	£100,000
	£250,000

What do you think The Banker's offer was?

A. £5,300   **B.** £2,100   **C.** £4,000

QUESTION 07
OPENING OFFERS

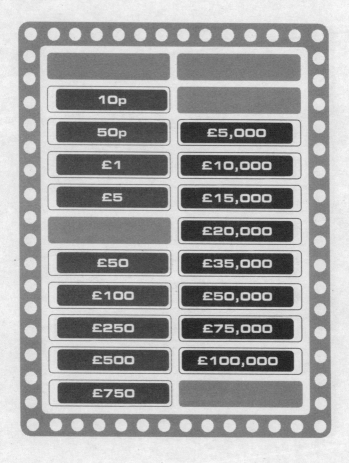

10p	
50p	£5,000
£1	£10,000
£5	£15,000
	£20,000
£50	£35,000
£100	£50,000
£250	£75,000
£500	£100,000
£750	

What do you think The Banker's offer was?

A. £10,200   **B.** £1,200   **C.** £6,600

QUESTION 08
OPENING OFFERS

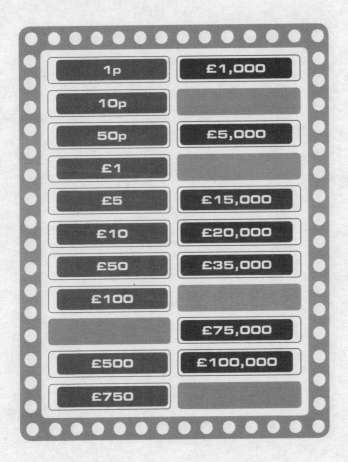

1p	£1,000
10p	
50p	£5,000
£1	
£5	£15,000
£10	£20,000
£50	£35,000
£100	
	£75,000
£500	£100,000
£750	

What do you think The Banker's offer was?

A. £700   **B.** £200   **C.** £1,600

QUESTION 09
OPENING OFFERS

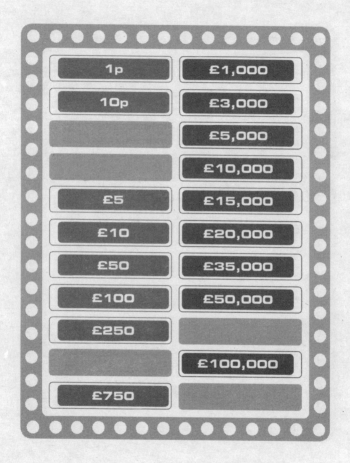

1p	£1,000
10p	£3,000
	£5,000
	£10,000
£5	£15,000
£10	£20,000
£50	£35,000
£100	£50,000
£250	
	£100,000
£750	

What do you think The Banker's offer was?

A. £12,000   **B.** £15,000   **C.** £1,300

QUESTION 10
OPENING OFFERS

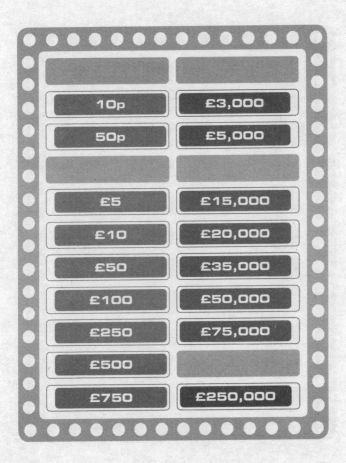

10p	£3,000
50p	£5,000
£5	£15,000
£10	£20,000
£50	£35,000
£100	£50,000
£250	£75,000
£500	
£750	£250,000

What do you think The Banker's offer was?

A. £14,400   **B.** £2,000   **C.** £7,000

QUESTION 11
OPENING OFFERS

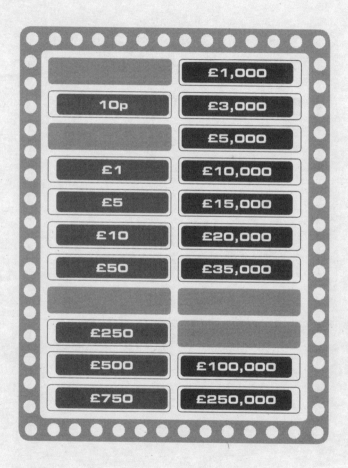

	£1,000
10p	£3,000
	£5,000
£1	£10,000
£5	£15,000
£10	£20,000
£50	£35,000
£250	
£500	£100,000
£750	£250,000

What do you think The Banker's offer was?

A. £8,600   **B.** £4,700   **C.** £1,300

QUESTION 12
OPENING OFFERS

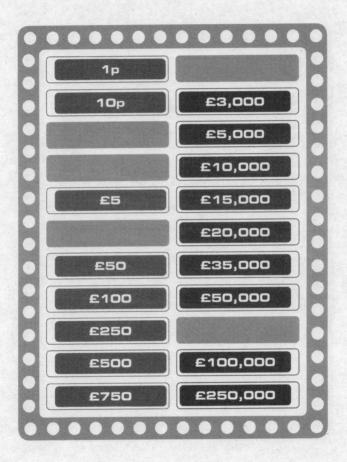

1p	
10p	£3,000
	£5,000
	£10,000
£5	£15,000
	£20,000
£50	£35,000
£100	£50,000
£250	
£500	£100,000
£750	£250,000

What do you think The Banker's offer was?

A. £2,000   **B.** £3,300   **C.** £5,600

QUESTION 13
OPENING OFFERS

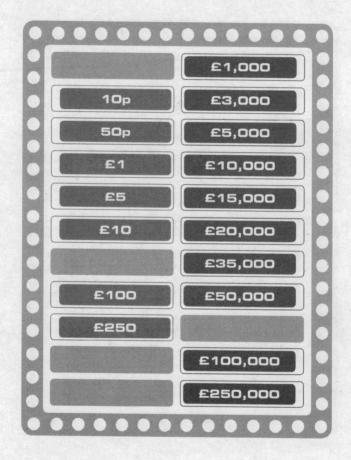

	£1,000
10p	£3,000
50p	£5,000
£1	£10,000
£5	£15,000
£10	£20,000
	£35,000
£100	£50,000
£250	
	£100,000
	£250,000

What do you think The Banker's offer was?

A. £3,100   **B.** £8,000   **C.** £12,900

QUESTION 14
OPENING OFFERS

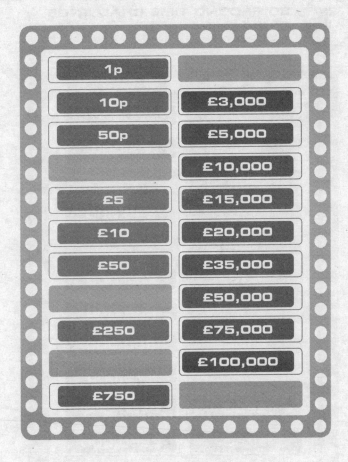

1p	
10p	£3,000
50p	£5,000
	£10,000
£5	£15,000
£10	£20,000
£50	£35,000
	£50,000
£250	£75,000
	£100,000
£750	

What do you think The Banker's offer was?

A. £6,500   **B.** £2,500   **C.** £500

QUESTION 15
OPENING OFFERS

 30 SECOND TIME CHALLENGE
Try and answer this question
in 30 seconds.

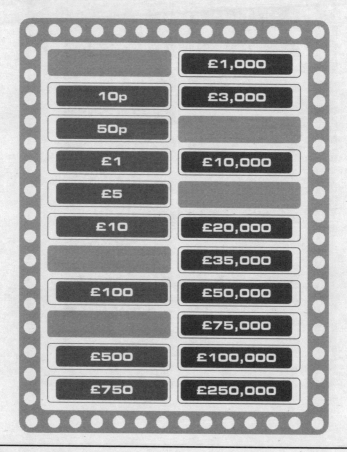

	£1,000
10p	£3,000
50p	
£1	£10,000
£5	
£10	£20,000
	£35,000
£100	£50,000
	£75,000
£500	£100,000
£750	£250,000

What do you think The Banker's offer was?

A. £4,100   **B.** £9,000   **C.** £1,200

24

QUESTION 16
OPENING OFFERS

30 SECOND TIME CHALLENGE
Try and answer this question
in 30 seconds.

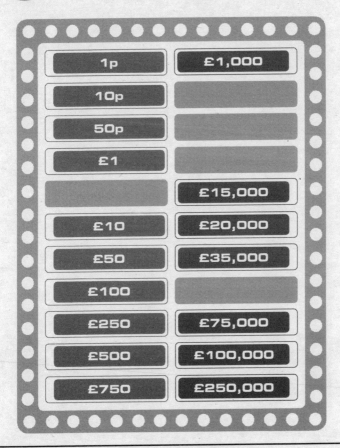

1p	£1,000
10p	
50p	
£1	
	£15,000
£10	£20,000
£50	£35,000
£100	
£250	£75,000
£500	£100,000
£750	£250,000

What do you think The Banker's offer was?

A. £3,000   **B.** £6,900   **C.** £10,500

ANSWERS
OPENING OFFERS

Circle your answers here, then check on page 384 to see how many you got correct.

GAME 01	**A.** £4,300	**B.** £52,800	**C.** £11,000
GAME 02	**A.** £95,000	**B.** £50	**C.** £3,100
GAME 03	**A.** £1,100	**B.** £8,000	**C.** £70,000
GAME 04	**A.** £8,700	**B.** £6,300	**C.** £12,000
GAME 05	**A.** £800	**B.** £200	**C.** £100
GAME 06	**A.** £5,300	**B.** £2,100	**C.** £4,000
GAME 07	**A.** £10,200	**B.** £1,200	**C.** £6,600
GAME 08	**A.** £700	**B.** £200	**C.** £1,600
GAME 09	**A.** £12,000	**B.** £15,000	**C.** £1,300
GAME 10	**A.** £14,400	**B.** £2,000	**C.** £7,000
GAME 11	**A.** £8,600	**B.** £4,700	**C.** £1,300
GAME 12	**A.** £2,000	**B.** £3,300	**C.** £5,600
GAME 13	**A.** £3,100	**B.** £8,000	**C.** £12,900
GAME 14	**A.** £6,500	**B.** £2,500	**C.** £500
GAME 15	**A.** £4,100	**B.** £9,000	**C.** £1,200
GAME 16	**A.** £3,000	**B.** £6,900	**C.** £10,500

CHAPTER 02
GUESS THE NEXT OFFER:
BEGINNER

I hope you did well in Chapter 1. You should be getting the hang of things by now, so in this chapter we're going to step up the pace a little. We're going to take you through the first three rounds of a real game to let you see how it develops and then ask you a multiple choice question about The Banker's next offer.

This part is for beginners, so it shouldn't give you too much trouble, but remember you have to start trying to think like him. He's smart, but so are you, and the lessons you are learning now will help you in the later chapters. Study him. What's his strategy? He will have one, you can be sure of that. Is he being generous, or just cunning? These were real games, so maybe you can spot a pattern in the way it was played. Was the contestant nervous, or rash?

Circle your answers as before and then fill them in at the end to see how you got on. The Banker will be there too to give you his opinion. Good luck!

GAME 01

CONTESTANT'S BOX 14

£1	£1k	£15k	£20k	£250k
4	3	1	8	22

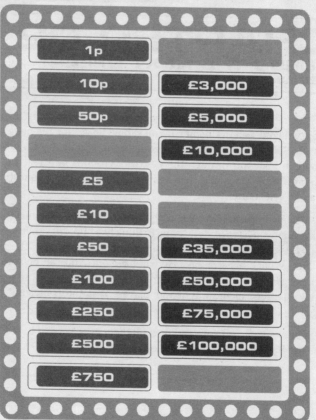

1p	
10p	£3,000
50p	£5,000
	£10,000
£5	
£10	
£50	£35,000
£100	£50,000
£250	£75,000
£500	£100,000
£750	

BANKER'S OFFER
£500

X NO DEAL

32

1p	£5	£100
2	16	19

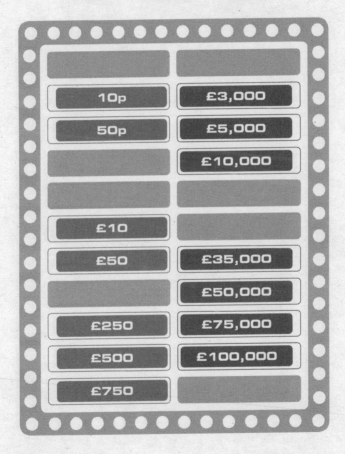

10p	£3,000
50p	£5,000
	£10,000
£10	
£50	£35,000
	£50,000
£250	£75,000
£500	£100,000
£750	

BANKER'S OFFER
£1,000

X NO DEAL

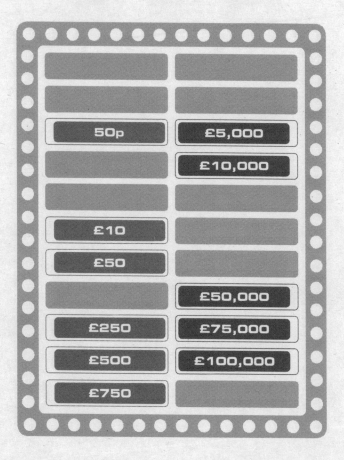

50p	£5,000
	£10,000
£10	
£50	
	£50,000
£250	£75,000
£500	£100,000
£750	

BANKER'S OFFER
£1,900

X NO DEAL

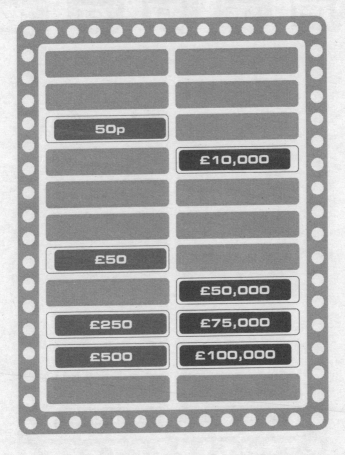

What do you think The Banker's offer was?

A. £25,000   **B.** £32,000   **C.** £7,300

35

GAME 02
CONTESTANT'S BOX

12

£1	£50	£1k	£20k	£35k
14	13	6	21	17

1p	
10p	£3,000
50p	£5,000
	£10,000
£5	£15,000
£10	
£100	£50,000
£250	£75,000
£500	£100,000
£750	£250,000

BANKER'S OFFER
£1,400

X NO DEAL

36

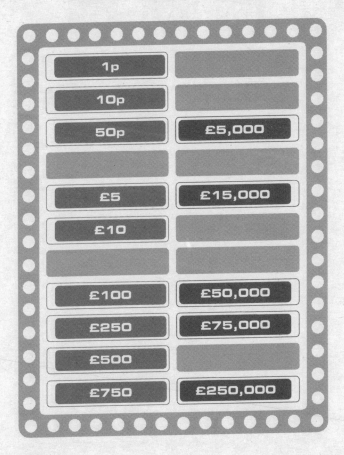

1p	
10p	
50p	£5,000
£5	£15,000
£10	
£100	£50,000
£250	£75,000
£500	
£750	£250,000

BANKER'S OFFER
£600

X NO DEAL

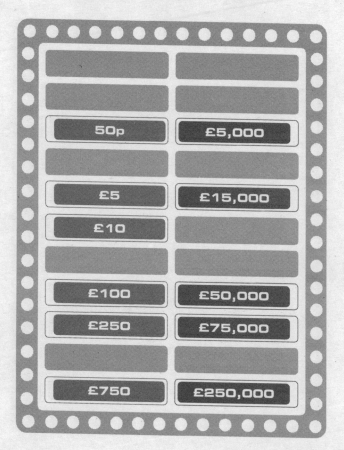

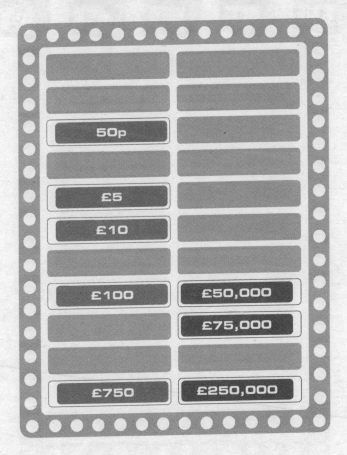

50p	
£5	
£10	
£100	£50,000
	£75,000
£750	£250,000

What do you think The Banker's offer was?

A. £10,000   **B.** £20,000   **C.** £30,000

GAME 03
CONTESTANT'S BOX

15

£10k	£35k	£50k	£75k	£250k
11	1	3	8	9

1p	£1,000
10p	£3,000
50p	£5,000
£1	
£5	£15,000
£10	£20,000
£50	
£100	
£250	
£500	£100,000
£750	

BANKER'S OFFER
£1,700

X NO DEAL

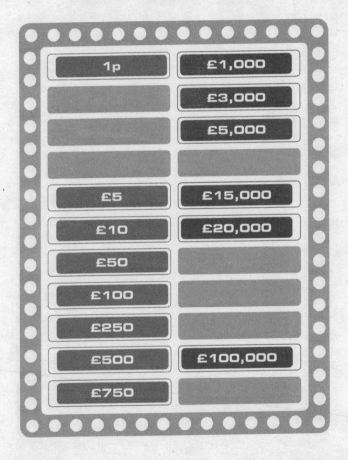

BANKER'S OFFER
£2,400

X NO DEAL

41

£100	£1k	£20k
2	12	5

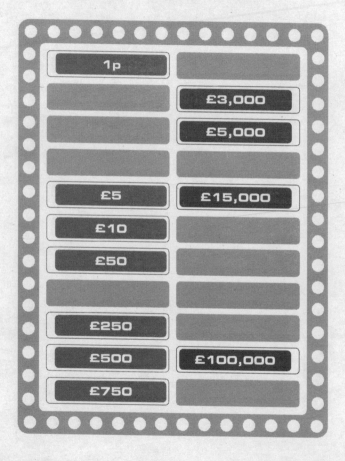

1p	
	£3,000
	£5,000
£5	£15,000
£10	
£50	
£250	
£500	£100,000
£750	

BANKER'S OFFER
£2,000

X NO DEAL

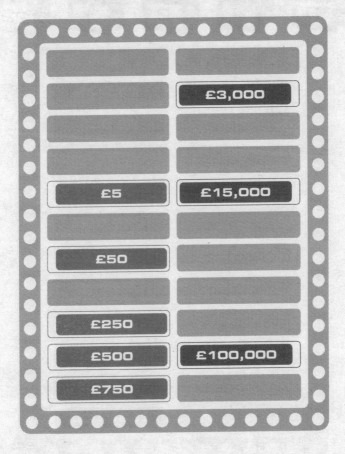

What do you think The Banker's offer was?

A. £4,700   **B.** £500   **C.** £1,000

£5	£500	£750	£5k	£50k
8	4	9	1	22

1p	£1,000
10p	£3,000
50p	
£1	£10,000
	£15,000
£10	£20,000
£50	£35,000
£100	
£250	£75,000
	£100,000
	£250,000

BANKER'S OFFER
£1,300

X NO DEAL

44

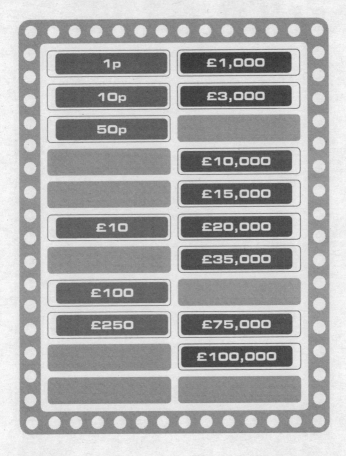

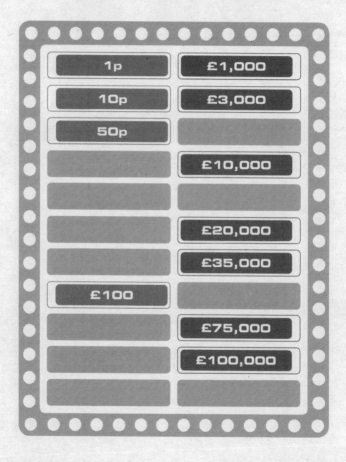

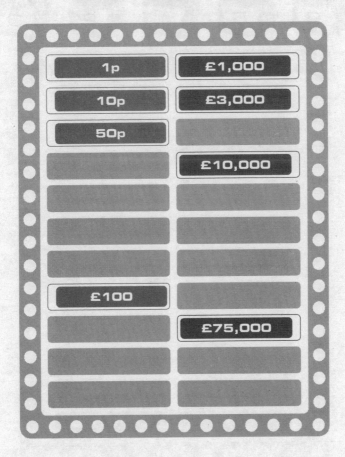

What do you think The Banker's offer was?

A. £9,500   **B.** £4,500   **C.** £10,000

GAME 05
CONTESTANT'S BOX

17

50p	£1	£250	£20k	£35k
9	6	1	2	3

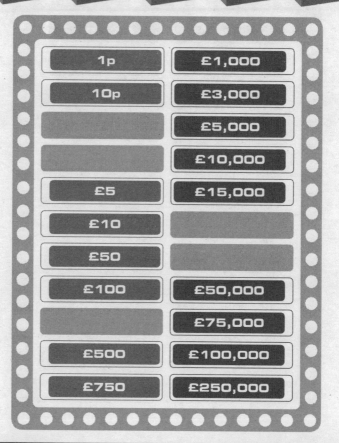

1p	£1,000
10p	£3,000
	£5,000
	£10,000
£5	£15,000
£10	
£50	
£100	
	£50,000
	£75,000
£500	£100,000
£750	£250,000

BANKER'S OFFER
£3,400

X NO DEAL

48

	£1,000
10p	£3,000
	£10,000
£5	£15,000
£10	
£50	
£100	£50,000
	£75,000
£500	£100,000
	£250,000

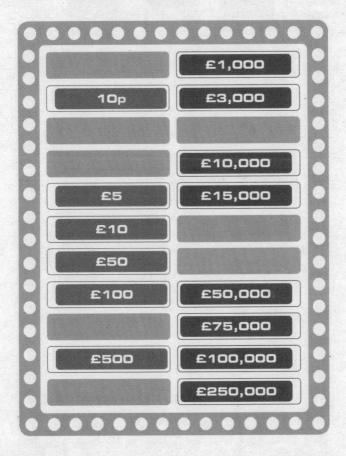

BANKER'S OFFER
£8,100

X NO DEAL

£50	£500	£15k
7	21	4

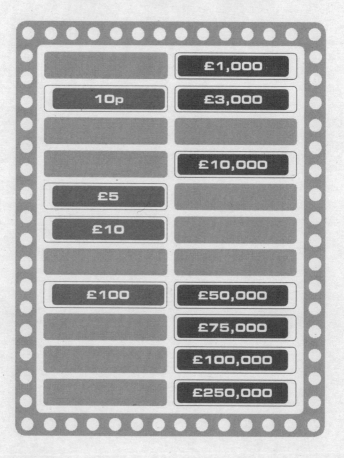

	£1,000
10p	£3,000
	£10,000
£5	
£10	
£100	£50,000
	£75,000
	£100,000
	£250,000

BANKER'S OFFER
£26,000

✗ NO DEAL

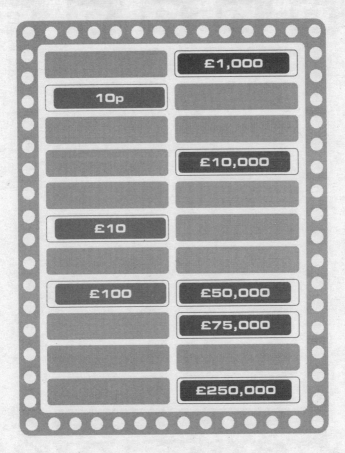

£1,000

10p

£10,000

£10

£100   £50,000

£75,000

£250,000

What do you think The Banker's offer was?

A. £42,000   **B.** £28,000   **C.** £50,000

51

GAME 06
CONTESTANT'S BOX

21

£1	£5	£3k	£35k	£50k
5	4	3	1	2

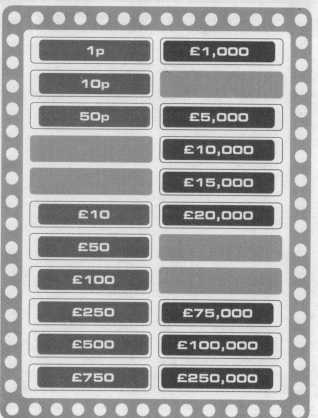

1p	£1,000
10p	
50p	£5,000
	£10,000
	£15,000
£10	£20,000
£50	
£100	
£250	£75,000
£500	£100,000
£750	£250,000

BANKER'S OFFER
£4,321

X NO DEAL

52

1p	
10p	
50p	£5,000
	£15,000
£10	
£50	
£100	
£250	£75,000
£500	£100,000
£750	£250,000

BANKER'S OFFER
£900

X NO DEAL

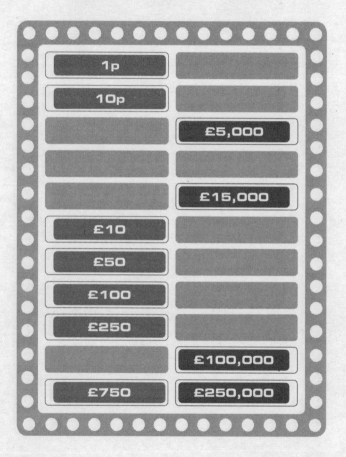

1p	
10p	
	£5,000
	£15,000
£10	
£50	
£100	
£250	
	£100,000
£750	£250,000

 BANKER'S OFFER £600

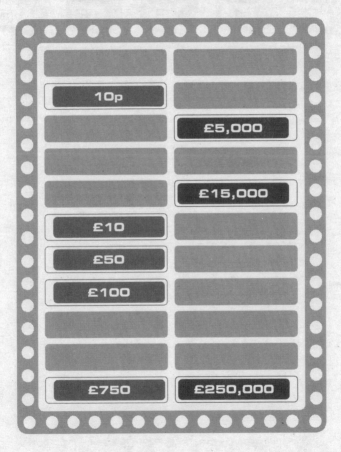

What do you think The Banker's offer was?

A. £20,000   **B.** £4,321   **C.** £12,000

GAME 07

CONTESTANT'S BOX 5

£10	£250	£750	£5k	£250k
7	1	3	16	15

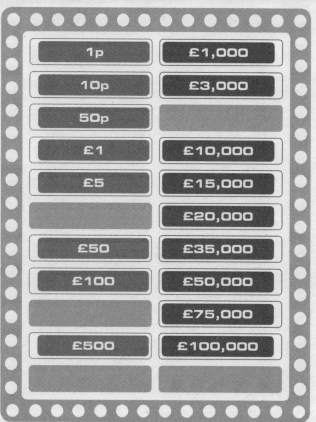

1p	£1,000
10p	£3,000
50p	
£1	£10,000
£5	£15,000
	£20,000
£50	£35,000
£100	£50,000
	£75,000
£500	£100,000

BANKER'S OFFER
£2,200

X NO DEAL

56

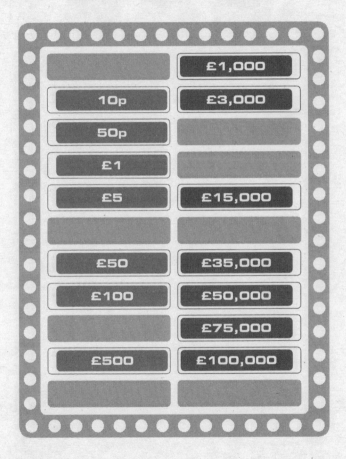

 BANKER'S OFFER £2,200

10p	£3,000
50p	
£5	£15,000
£50	£35,000
£100	£50,000
	£75,000
	£100,000

BANKER'S OFFER £8,400

X NO DEAL

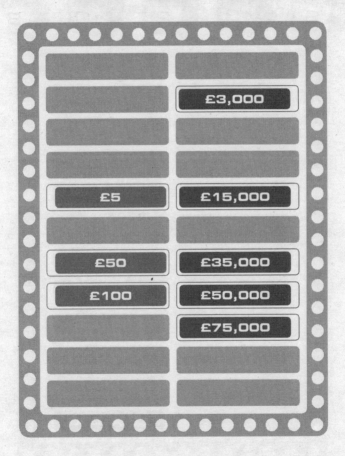

What do you think The Banker's offer was?

A. £6,000   **B.** £600   **C.** £60,000

10p	50p	£750	£15k	£100k
6	13	2	10	8

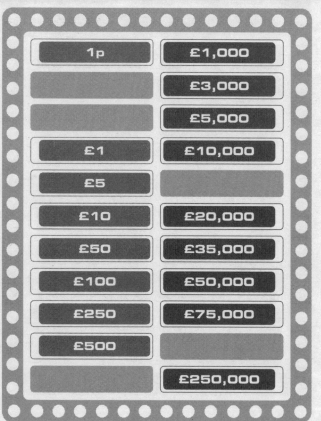

1p	£1,000
	£3,000
	£5,000
£1	£10,000
£5	
£10	£20,000
£50	£35,000
£100	£50,000
£250	£75,000
£500	
	£250,000

BANKER'S OFFER
£3,600

✗ NO DEAL

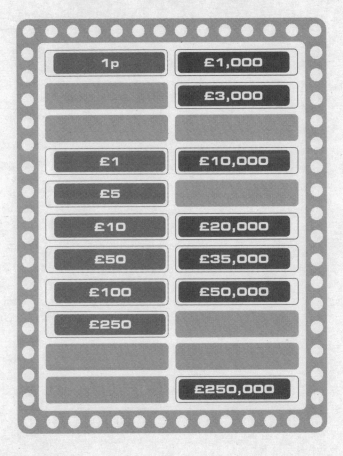

1p	£1,000
	£3,000
£1	£10,000
£5	
£10	£20,000
£50	£35,000
£100	£50,000
£250	
	£250,000

BANKER'S OFFER
£4,000

X NO DEAL

61

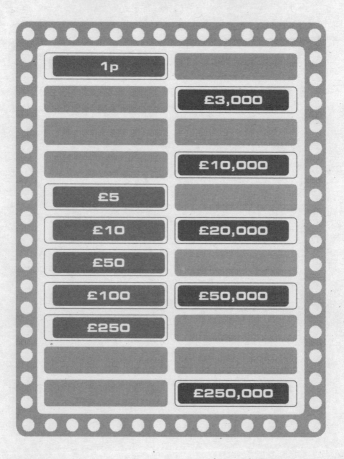

1p	
	£3,000
	£10,000
£5	
£10	£20,000
£50	
£100	£50,000
£250	
	£250,000

BANKER'S OFFER
£9,900

X NO DEAL

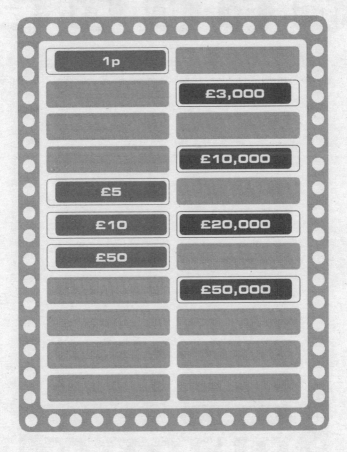

1p	
	£3,000
	£10,000
£5	
£10	£20,000
£50	
	£50,000

What do you think The Banker's offer was?

A. £12,000   **B.** £3,000   **C.** £6,000

63

50p	£50	£100	£50k	£250k
13	10	15	6	7

1p	£1,000
10p	£3,000
	£5,000
£1	£10,000
£5	£15,000
£10	£20,000
	£35,000
£250	£75,000
£500	£100,000
£750	

BANKER'S OFFER
£2,500

X NO DEAL

64

30 SECOND TIME CHALLENGE
Try and answer this question
in 30 seconds.

£250	£35k	£75k
22	1	18

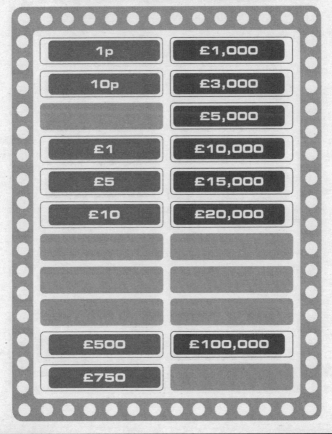

1p	£1,000
10p	£3,000
	£5,000
£1	£10,000
£5	£15,000
£10	£20,000
£500	£100,000
£750	

BANKER'S OFFER
£900

X NO DEAL

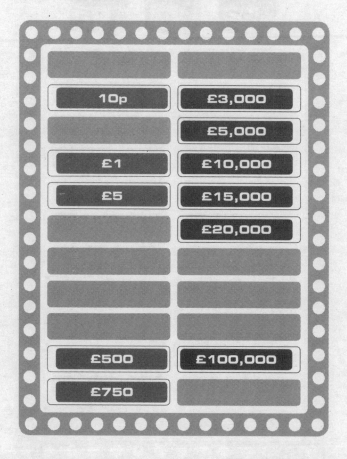

BANKER'S OFFER
£3,600

X NO DEAL

66

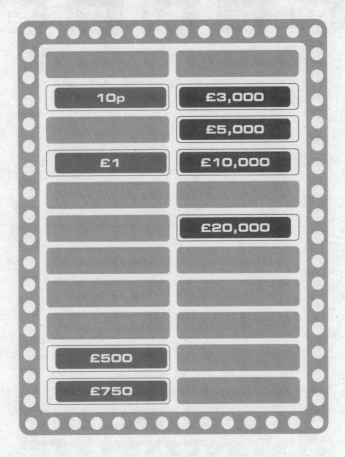

10p	£3,000
	£5,000
£1	£10,000
	£20,000
£500	
£750	

What do you think The Banker's offer was?

A. £1,300   **B.** £14,500   **C.** £18,000

GAME 10
CONTESTANT'S BOX

| 1 |

1p	£250	£750	£5k	£15k
10	17	7	14	3

	£1,000
10p	£3,000
50p	
£1	£10,000
£5	
£10	£20,000
£50	£35,000
£100	£50,000
	£75,000
£500	£100,000
	£250,000

BANKER'S OFFER
£500

X NO DEAL

£100	£1k	£250k
4	21	6

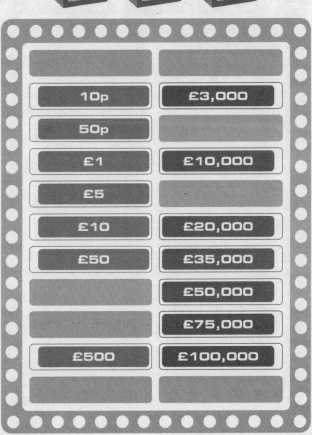

10p	£3,000
50p	
£1	£10,000
£5	
£10	£20,000
£50	£35,000
	£50,000
	£75,000
£500	£100,000

BANKER'S OFFER
£3,100

X NO DEAL

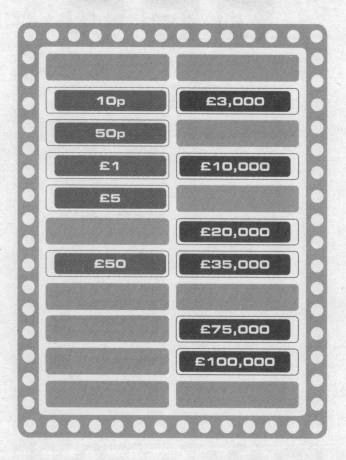

10p	£3,000
50p	
£1	£10,000
£5	
	£20,000
£50	£35,000
	£75,000
	£100,000

BANKER'S OFFER
£6,700

X NO DEAL

70

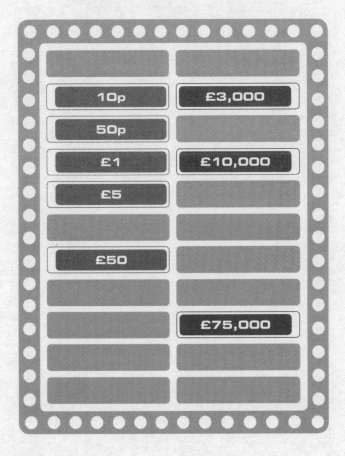

What do you think The Banker's offer was?

A. £5,000   **B.** £21,000   **C.** £1,500

ANSWERS
GUESS THE NEXT OFFER
BEGINNER

Circle your answers here, then check on page 386 to see how many you got correct.

GAME 01	**A.** £25,000	**B.** £32,000	**C.** £7,300
GAME 02	**A.** £10,000	**B.** £20,000	**C.** £30,000
GAME 03	**A.** £4,700	**B.** £500	**C.** £1,000
GAME 04	**A.** £9,500	**B.** £4,500	**C.** £10,000
GAME 05	**A.** £42,000	**B.** £28,000	**C.** £50,000
GAME 06	**A.** £20,000	**B.** £4,321	**C.** £12,000
GAME 07	**A.** £6,000	**B.** £600	**C.** £60,000
GAME 08	**A.** £12,000	**B.** £3,000	**C.** £6,000
GAME 09	**A.** £1,300	**B.** £14,500	**C.** £18,000
GAME 10	**A.** £5,000	**B.** £21,000	**C.** £1,500

CHAPTER 03
GUESS THE NEXT OFFER:
EXPERT

Well, that last chapter should have taught you a lot about how The Banker thinks and what he's going to do next. But be careful. Many contestants have thought they had got him all figured out, only to come a cropper when something unexpected happened. He likes to surprise people, and he mostly does.

We are going to move now onto the expert version of the last game and the tension is beginning to mount. With every chapter things get more serious.

In the studio, it's getting hot. But The Banker is as cool as a cucumber, be sure of that. So stay calm, and don't rush into any decisions – not easy when you're against the clock in the last two games, I know, but The Banker never panics. He might pretend to, sometimes, but he always plays the board by the numbers. And that's exacly what you've got to do. Don't be put off if the money is big, play the game and try to guess what he'd do next. That's how you'll win. You won't if you ignore the run of play and just go for whatever seems best.

Circle your answers as before and tot them up at the end. The Banker will be waiting. Off you go, there's the phone...

GAME 01
CONTESTANT'S BOX

11

50p	£50	£100	£15k	£250k
21	1	20	19	7

1p	£1,000
10p	£3,000
	£5,000
£1	£10,000
£5	
£10	£20,000
	£35,000
	£50,000
£250	£75,000
£500	£100,000
£750	

BANKER'S OFFER
£2,300

X NO DEAL

78

| 12 | £5 | 8 | £75k | 16 | £100k |

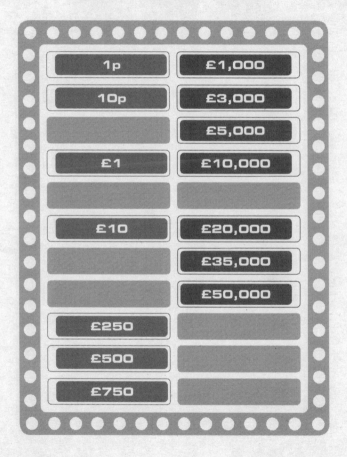

1p	£1,000
10p	£3,000
	£5,000
£1	£10,000
£10	£20,000
	£35,000
	£50,000
£250	
£500	
£750	

BANKER'S OFFER
£1,900

X NO DEAL

£500 6 | £3k 18 | £5k 13

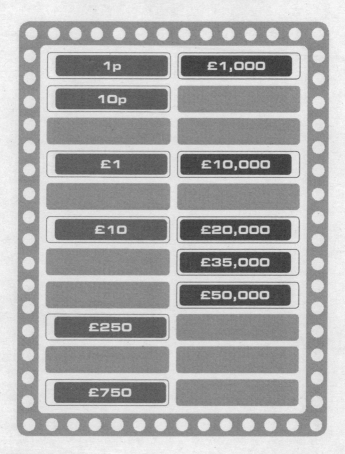

1p	£1,000
10p	
£1	£10,000
£10	£20,000
	£35,000
	£50,000
£250	
£750	

BANKER'S OFFER
£8,900

X NO DEAL

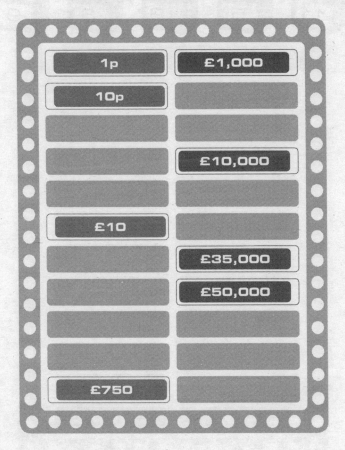

1p	£1,000
10p	
	£10,000
£10	
	£35,000
	£50,000
£750	

What do you think The Banker's offer was?

A. £8,900   **B.** £9,900   **C.** £6,400

81

GAME 02
CONTESTANT'S BOX

10

£1 — 11
£250 — 5
£500 — 19
£1k — 6
£3k — 9

1p	
10p	
50p	£5,000
	£10,000
£5	£15,000
£10	£20,000
£50	£35,000
£100	£50,000
	£75,000
	£100,000
£750	£250,000

BANKER'S OFFER
£7,100

X NO DEAL

82

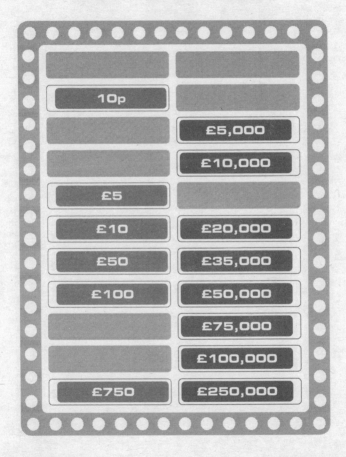

10p	
	£5,000
	£10,000
£5	
£10	£20,000
£50	£35,000
£100	£50,000
	£75,000
	£100,000
£750	£250,000

BANKER'S OFFER
£14,900

✕ NO DEAL

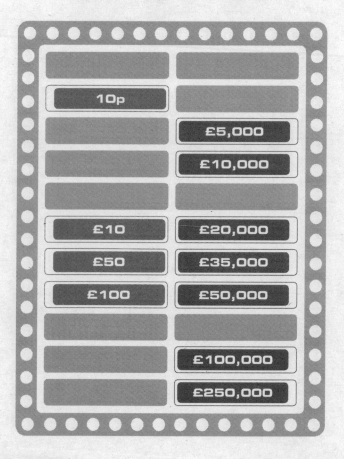

10p	
	£5,000
	£10,000
£10	£20,000
£50	£35,000
£100	£50,000
	£100,000
	£250,000

 BANKER'S OFFER £16,000

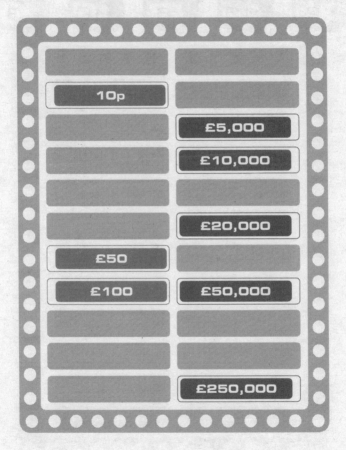

10p	
	£5,000
	£10,000
	£20,000
£50	
£100	£50,000
	£250,000

What do you think The Banker's offer was?

A. £12,000 **B.** £7,100 **C.** £17,000

GAME 03

CONTESTANT'S BOX

9

£100	£250	£3k	£15k	£75k
2	13	6	10	3

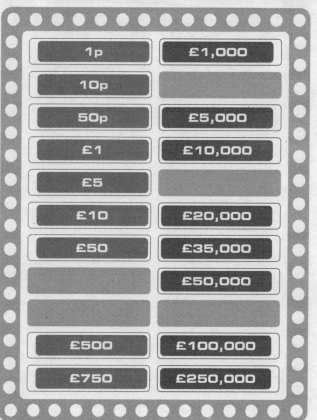

1p	£1,000
10p	
50p	£5,000
£1	£10,000
£5	
£10	£20,000
£50	£35,000
	£50,000
£500	£100,000
£750	£250,000

BANKER'S OFFER
£2,400

X **NO DEAL**

£1	£50	£50k
15	5	7

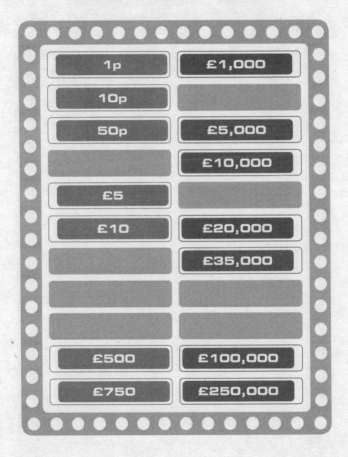

1p	£1,000
10p	
50p	£5,000
	£10,000
£5	
£10	£20,000
	£35,000
£500	£100,000
£750	£250,000

BANKER'S OFFER
£6,800

X NO DEAL

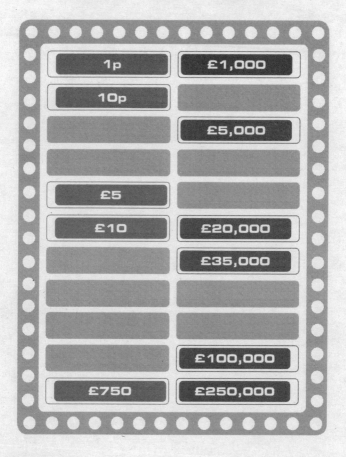

1p	£1,000
10p	
	£5,000
£5	
£10	£20,000
	£35,000
	£100,000
£750	£250,000

BANKER'S OFFER
£13,000

X NO DEAL

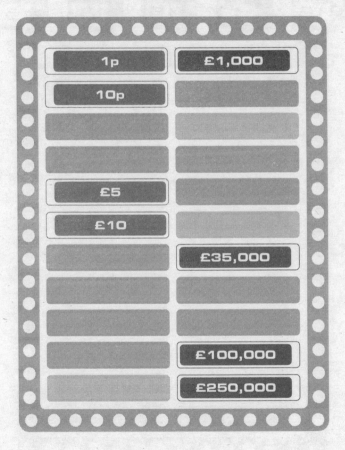

What do you think The Banker's offer was?

A. £21,000   **B.** £18,000   **C.** £24,000

1p	£35k	£50k	£75k	£250k
16	1	15	6	5

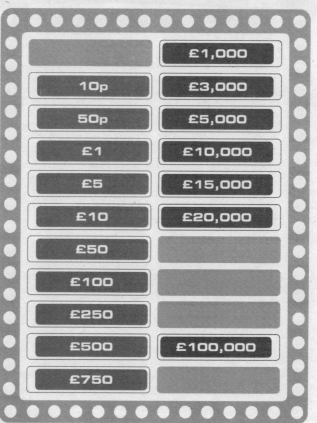

	£1,000
10p	£3,000
50p	£5,000
£1	£10,000
£5	£15,000
£10	£20,000
£50	
£100	
£250	
£500	£100,000
£750	

BANKER'S OFFER
£220

X NO DEAL

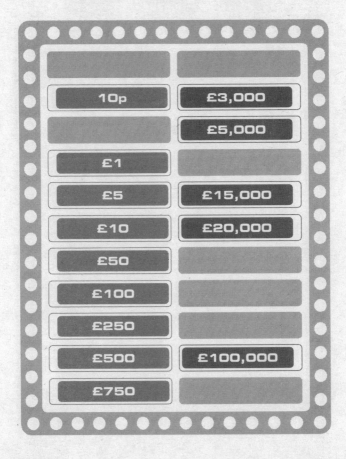

10p	£3,000
	£5,000
£1	
£5	£15,000
£10	£20,000
£50	
£100	
£250	
£500	£100,000
£750	

BANKER'S OFFER
2,200

X NO DEAL

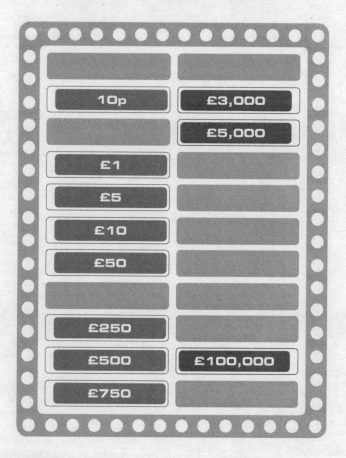

10p	£3,000
	£5,000
£1	
£5	
£10	
£50	
£250	
£500	£100,000
£750	

BANKER'S OFFER £2,500

✗ NO DEAL

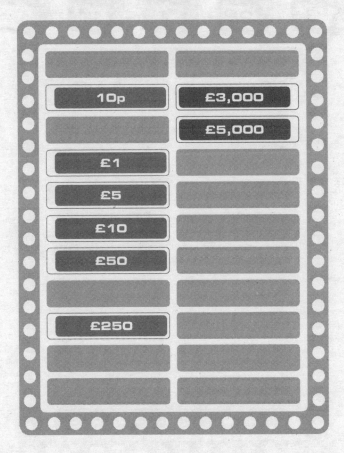

10p	£3,000
	£5,000
£1	
£5	
£10	
£50	
£250	

What do you think The Banker's offer was?

A. £220   **B.** £400   **C.** £380

50p	£1k	£10k	£50k	£100k
3	22	1	11	7

1p	
10p	£3,000
	£5,000
£1	
£5	£15,000
£10	£20,000
£50	£35,000
£100	
£250	£75,000
£500	
£750	£250,000

BANKER'S OFFER
£3,300

X NO DEAL

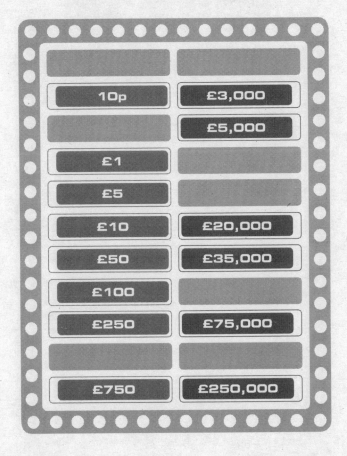

BANKER'S OFFER
£5,900

X NO DEAL

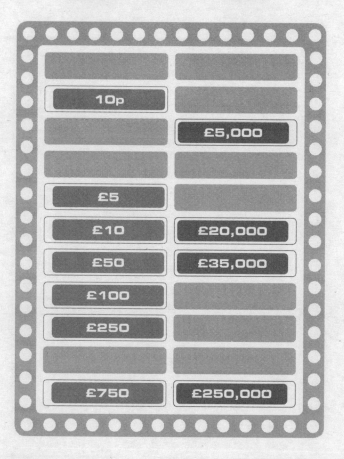

10p	
	£5,000
£5	
£10	£20,000
£50	£35,000
£100	
£250	
£750	£250,000

BANKER'S OFFER **£8,000**   ✗ **NO DEAL**

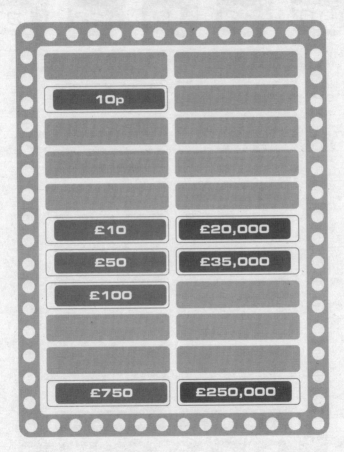

What do you think The Banker's offer was?

A. £12,000   **B.** £24,000   **C.** £18,000

GAME 06

CONTESTANT'S BOX 18

1p 10	10p 12	£100 5	£10k 22	£100k 3

	£1,000
	£3,000
50p	£5,000
£1	
£5	£15,000
£10	£20,000
£50	£35,000
	£50,000
£250	£75,000
£500	
£750	£250,000

BANKER'S OFFER
£2,800

X NO DEAL

	£1,000
50p	
£1	
£5	£15,000
	£20,000
£50	£35,000
	£50,000
£250	£75,000
£500	
£750	£250,000

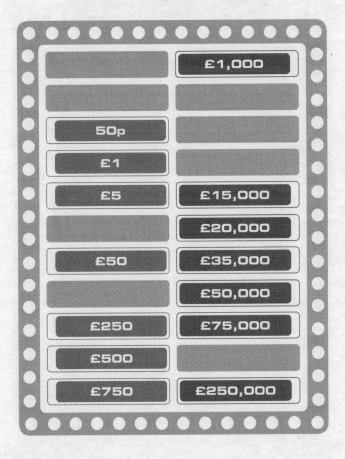

BANKER'S OFFER
£8,100

X NO DEAL

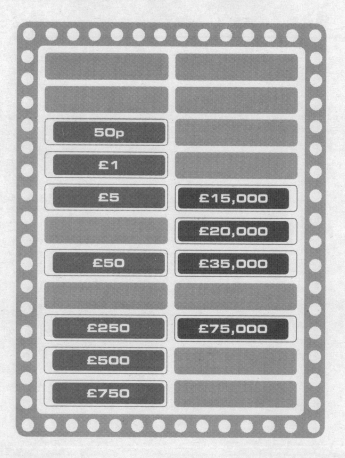

50p	
£1	
£5	£15,000
	£20,000
£50	£35,000
£250	£75,000
£500	
£750	

 BANKER'S OFFER **£1,600**   ✕ **NO DEAL**

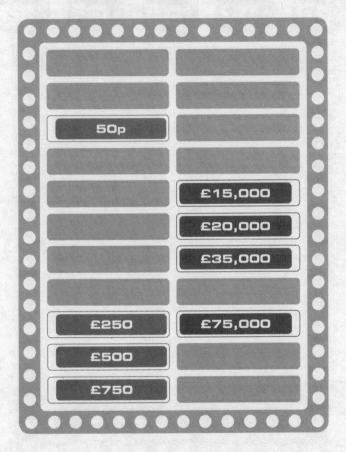

What do you think The Banker's offer was?

A. £7,200   **B.** £9,000   **C.** £10,000

GAME 07

CONTESTANT'S BOX 14

£100 — 21	£500 — 17	£10k — 16	£15k — 22	£50k — 2

1p	£1,000
10p	£3,000
50p	£5,000
£1	
£5	
£10	£20,000
£50	£35,000
£250	£75,000
	£100,000
£750	£250,000

 BANKER'S OFFER £3,000 ✗ NO DEAL

102

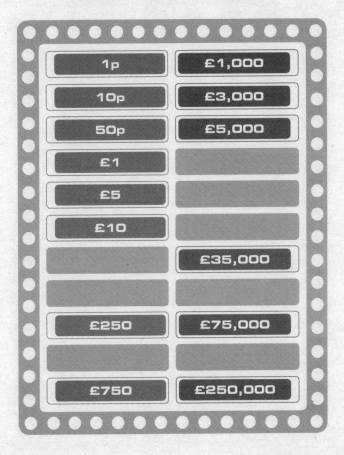

BANKER'S OFFER
£3,000

X NO DEAL

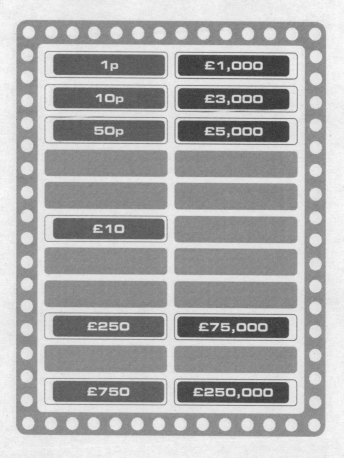

BANKER'S OFFER
£6,000

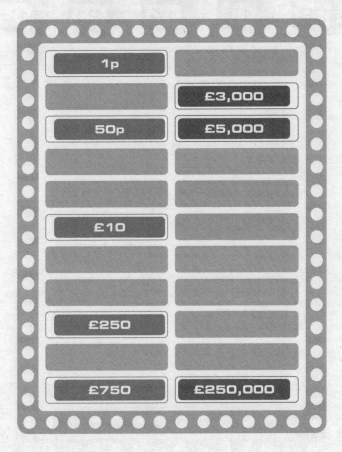

What do you think The Banker's offer was?

A. £8,000   **B.** £2000   **C.** £4,500

50p	£750	£1k	£5k	£100k
22	16	14	21	13

1p	
10p	£3,000
£1	£10,000
£5	£15,000
£10	£20,000
£50	£35,000
£100	£50,000
£250	£75,000
£500	
	£250,000

BANKER'S OFFER
£1,300

X NO DEAL

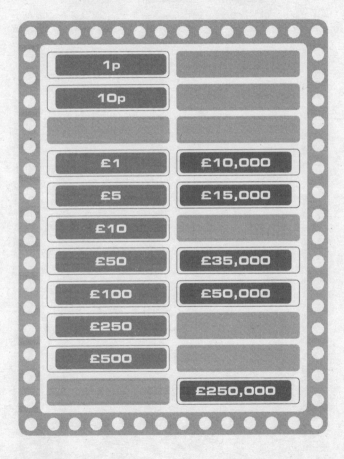

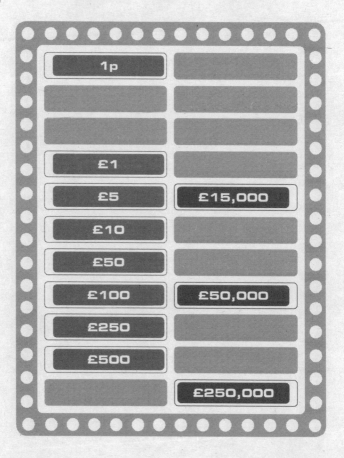

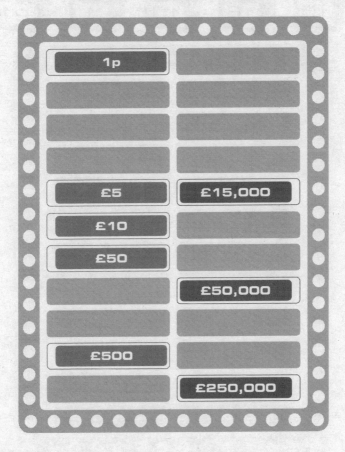

What do you think The Banker's offer was?

A. £7,100   **B.** £11,000   **C.** £14,500

50p	£50	£3k	£15k	£35k
15	16	10	1	21

1p	£1,000
10p	
	£5,000
£1	£10,000
£5	
£10	£20,000
£100	£50,000
£250	£75,000
£500	£100,000
£750	£250,000

BANKER'S OFFER
£4,000

X NO DEAL

1p — 4

£500 — 18

£75k — 5

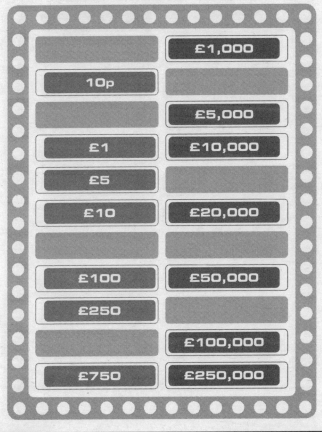

	£1,000
10p	
	£5,000
£1	£10,000
£5	
£10	£20,000
£100	£50,000
£250	
	£100,000
£750	£250,000

BANKER'S OFFER
£6,800

X NO DEAL

111

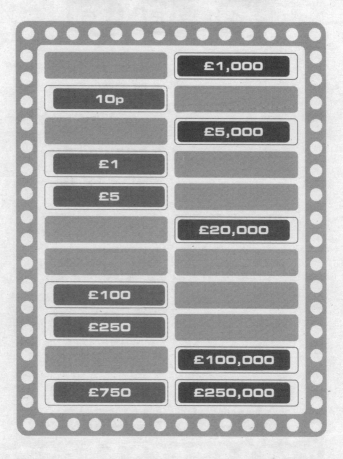

	£1,000
10p	
	£5,000
£1	
£5	
	£20,000
£100	
£250	
	£100,000
£750	£250,000

BANKER'S OFFER
£10,000

X NO DEAL

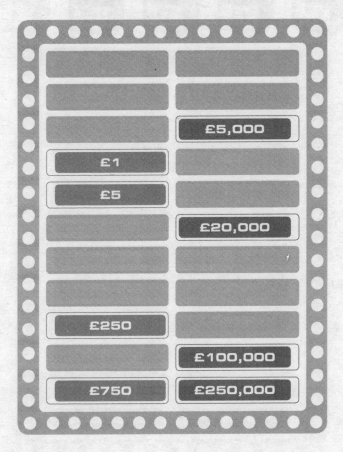

What do you think The Banker's offer was?

A. £13,500   **B.** £21,000   **C.** £19,000

GAME 10

CONTESTANT'S BOX

`4`

£500	£3k	£15k	£50	£100k
11	8	3	6	1

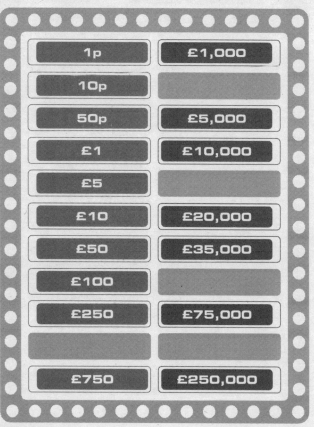

1p	£1,000
10p	
50p	£5,000
£1	£10,000
£5	
£10	£20,000
£50	£35,000
£100	
£250	£75,000
£750	£250,000

BANKER'S OFFER
£700

✗ NO DEAL

50p	£1k	£20k
15	19	9

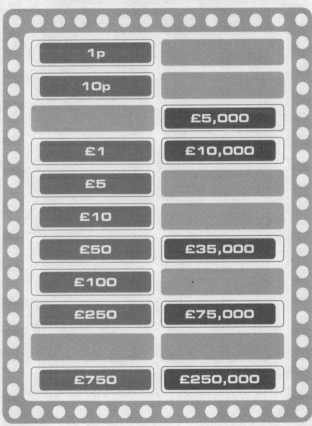

1p	
10p	
	£5,000
£1	£10,000
£5	
£10	
£50	£35,000
£100	
£250	£75,000
£750	£250,000

BANKER'S OFFER
£4,000

X **NO DEAL**

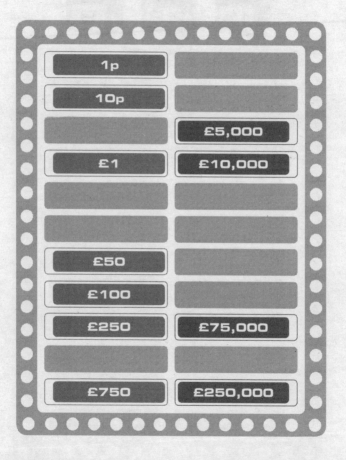

BANKER'S OFFER
£6,000

✗ NO DEAL

116

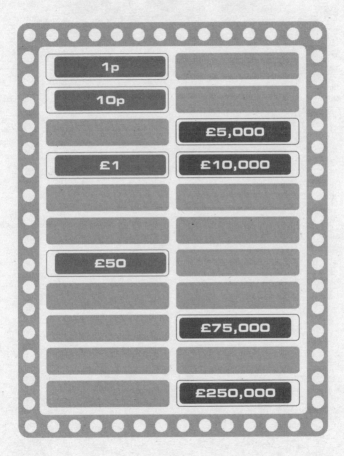

What do you think The Banker's offer was?

A. £17,800   **B.** £14,500   **C.** £19,400

117

ANSWERS
GUESS THE NEXT OFFER
EXPERT

Circle your answers here, then check on page 387 to see how many you got correct.

GAME 01	**A.** £8,900	**B.** £9,900	**C.** £6,400
GAME 02	**A.** £12,000	**B.** £7,100	**C.** £17,000
GAME 03	**A.** £21,000	**B.** £18,000	**C.** £24,000
GAME 04	**A.** £220	**B.** £400	**C.** £380
GAME 05	**A.** £12,000	**B.** £24,000	**C.** £18,000
GAME 06	**A.** £7,200	**B.** £9,000	**C.** £10,000
GAME 07	**A.** £8,000	**B.** £2,000	**C.** £4,500
GAME 08	**A.** £7,100	**B.** £11,000	**C.** £14,500
GAME 09	**A.** £13,500	**B.** £21,000	**C.** £19,000
GAME 10	**A.** £17,800	**B.** £14,500	**C.** £19,400

CHAPTER 04
TOTALISER:
BEGINNER

By now you should be really getting inside the game and maybe even starting to think like The Banker! I hope so, because now you're going to need everything you've learned so far.

In this chapter, and there's a harder version coming up in the next one, we're going to ask you to work out what the total of all The Banker's offers in one game added up to. To start you off we'll give you his first offer. This should help you get a feel for each game and allow you to plot the course of The Banker's twisted mind as he tries to keep his money and deny the contestant any chance of victory.

Try and follow him as he manoeuvres, going up, going down, sticking. What'll he do next? It's up to you to figure him out, outsmart him and take him down a peg or two. Keep disciplined, and think carefully about each question, don't go straight to the multiple choice. Each game has its own logic, it's there if you look for it. And don't get flustered when you're playing against the clock!

Fill in the scorecard at the end of the chapter then check your answers at the back of the book. Have you managed to get to The Banker, or is he the one doing the laughimg? Something's ringing. It's for you...

GAME 01
CONTESTANT'S BOX

10p	£10	£250	£500	£1k
1	2	17	15	11

21

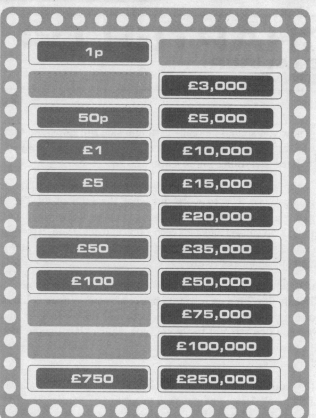

1p	
	£3,000
50p	£5,000
£1	£10,000
£5	£15,000
	£20,000
£50	£35,000
£100	£50,000
	£75,000
	£100,000
£750	£250,000

BANKER'S OFFER
£2,900

X NO DEAL

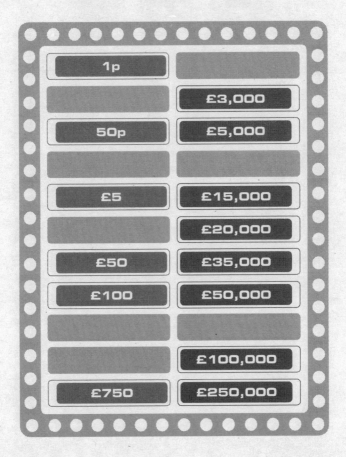

1p	
	£3,000
50p	£5,000
£5	£15,000
	£20,000
£50	£35,000
£100	£50,000
	£100,000
£750	£250,000

**What do you think
The Banker's offer was?**

....

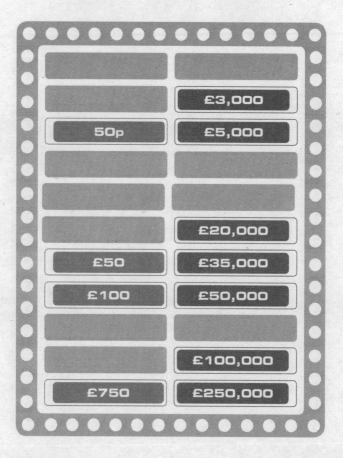

	£3,000
50p	£5,000
	£20,000
£50	£35,000
£100	£50,000
	£100,000
£750	£250,000

**What do you think
The Banker's offer was?**

....

126

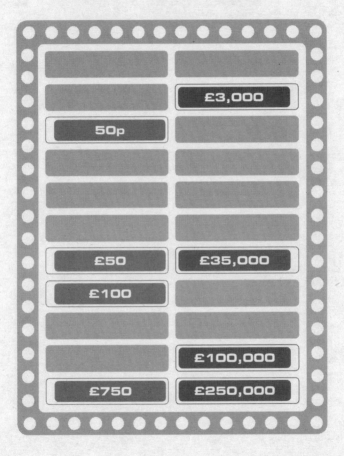

What do you think The Banker's offer was?

....

£50 £100 £100k
 6   14   5

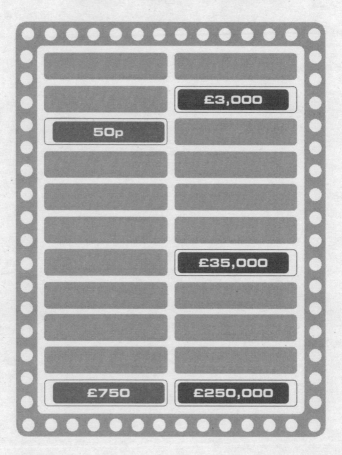

£3,000

50p

£35,000

£750   £250,000

What do you think
The Banker's offer was?

....

TOTALISER

ROUND	BANKER'S OFFERS
01	£2,900
02	
03	
04	
05	
TOTAL	

What total do you think The Banker's offers in this game (including the first round) add up to?

A. £73,400   **B.** £16,500   **C.** £198,400

£1	£5	£750	£1k	£20k
14	5	4	11	1

1p	
10p	£3,000
50p	£5,000
	£10,000
	£15,000
£10	
£50	£35,000
£100	£50,000
£250	£75,000
£500	£100,000
	£250,000

BANKER'S OFFER
£3,900

X **NO DEAL**

10p	£3,000
50p	
	£10,000
	£15,000
£10	
£50	£35,000
	£50,000
£250	£75,000
£500	£100,000
	£250,000

**What do you think
The Banker's offer was?**

....

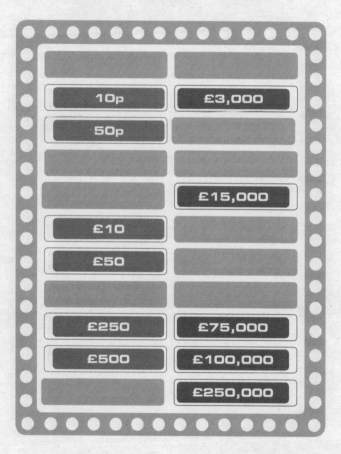

10p	£3,000
50p	
	£15,000
£10	
£50	
£250	£75,000
£500	£100,000
	£250,000

**What do you think
The Banker's offer was?**

....

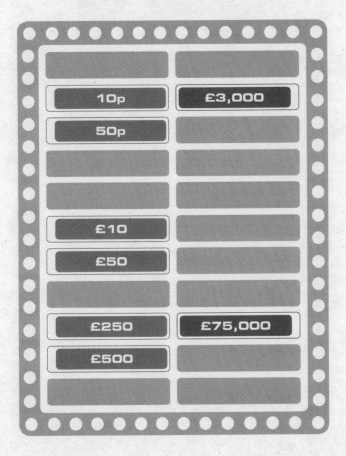

What do you think
The Banker's offer was?

....

133

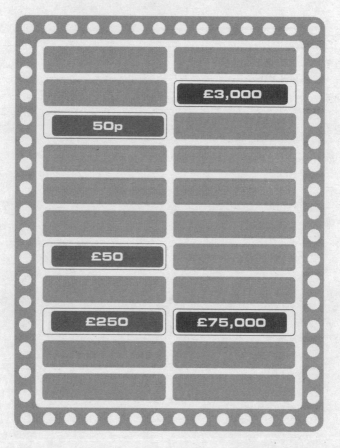

What do you think
The Banker's offer was?

....

134

TOTALISER

ROUND	BANKER'S OFFER
01	£3,900
02	
03	
04	
05	
TOTAL	

What total do you think The Banker's offers in this game (including the first round) **add up to?**

A. £53,800   **B.** £14,000   **C.** £99,700

1p	50p	£10	£35k	£50k
18	1	15	11	16

	£1,000
10p	£3,000
	£5,000
£1	£10,000
£5	£15,000
	£20,000
£50	
£100	
£250	£75,000
£500	£100,000
£750	£250,000

BANKER'S OFFER
£6,900

X **NO DEAL**

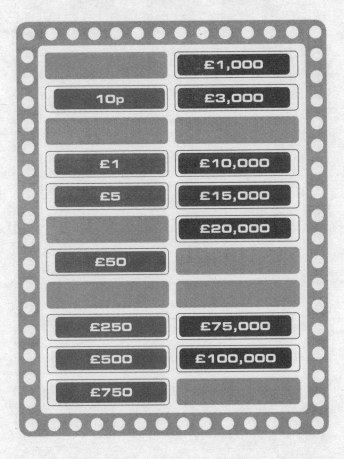

	£1,000
10p	£3,000
£1	£10,000
£5	£15,000
	£20,000
£50	
£250	£75,000
£500	£100,000
£750	

**What do you think
The Banker's offer was?**

....

137

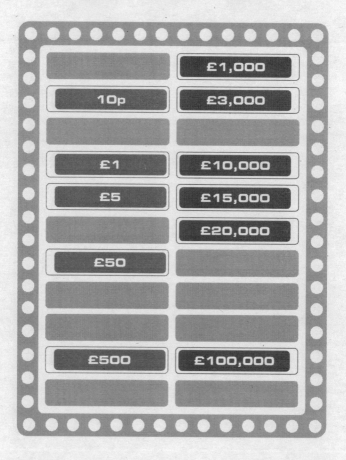

	£1,000
10p	£3,000
£1	£10,000
£5	£15,000
	£20,000
£50	
£500	£100,000

**What do you think
The Banker's offer was?**

....

138

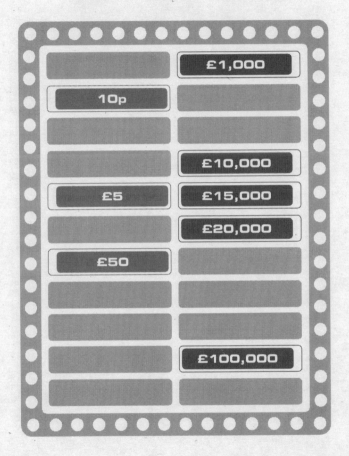

What do you think
The Banker's offer was?

....

139

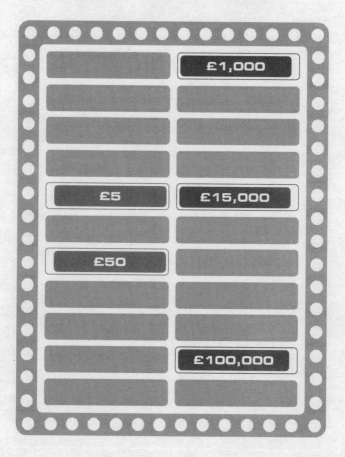

**What do you think
The Banker's offer was?**

....

140

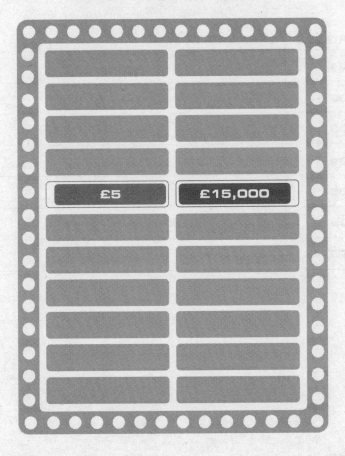

TOTALISER

ROUND	BANKER'S OFFER
01	£6,900
02	
03	
04	
05	
06	
TOTAL	

What total do you think The Banker's offers in this game (including the first round) add up to?

A. £24,200   **B.** £123,000   **C.** £60,900

1p	£50	£100	£50k	£250k
3	15	1	5	7

	£1,000
10p	£3,000
50p	£5,000
£1	£10,000
£5	£15,000
£10	£20,000
	£35,000
£250	£75,000
£500	£100,000
£750	

BANKER'S OFFER
£700

X NO DEAL

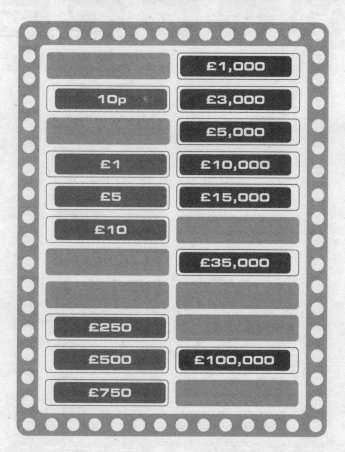

	£1,000
10p	£3,000
	£5,000
£1	£10,000
£5	£15,000
£10	
	£35,000
£250	
£500	£100,000
£750	

**What do you think
The Banker's offer was?**

....

144

	£1,000
10p	£3,000
	£5,000
£1	£10,000
	£15,000
	£35,000
£250	
	£100,000
£750	

What do you think The Banker's offer was?

....

145

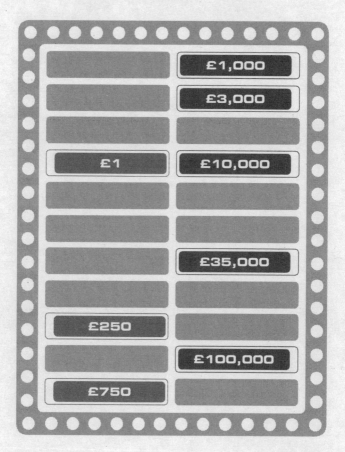

What do you think
The Banker's offer was?

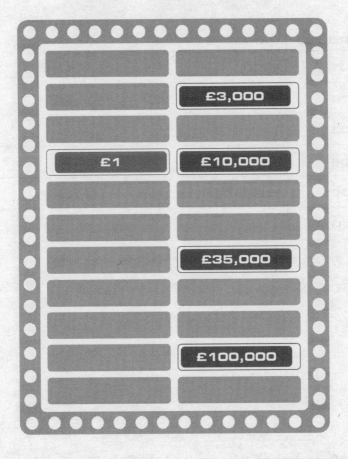

£3,000

£1   £10,000

£35,000

£100,000

**What do you think
The Banker's offer was?**

....

TOTALISER

ROUND	BANKER'S OFFER
01	£700
02	
03	
04	
05	
TOTAL	

What total do you think The Banker's offers in this game (including the first round) add up to?

A. £98,900   **B.** £1,300   **C.** £37,900

GAME 05

CONTESTANT'S BOX 9

1p	£10	£100	£3k	£35k
2	1	13	8	5

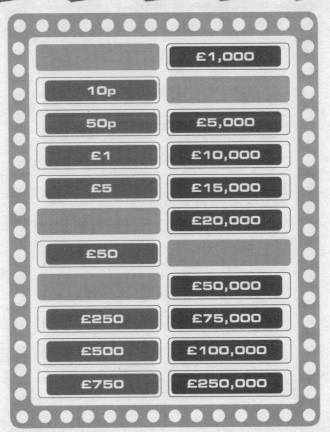

	£1,000
10p	
50p	£5,000
£1	£10,000
£5	£15,000
	£20,000
£50	
	£50,000
£250	£75,000
£500	£100,000
£750	£250,000

BANKER'S OFFER
£2,300

X NO DEAL

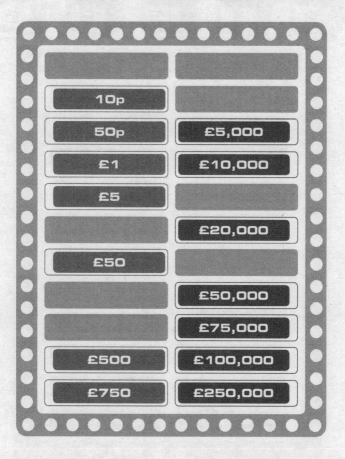

10p	
50p	£5,000
£1	£10,000
£5	
	£20,000
£50	
	£50,000
	£75,000
£500	£100,000
£750	£250,000

**What do you think
The Banker's offer was?**

....

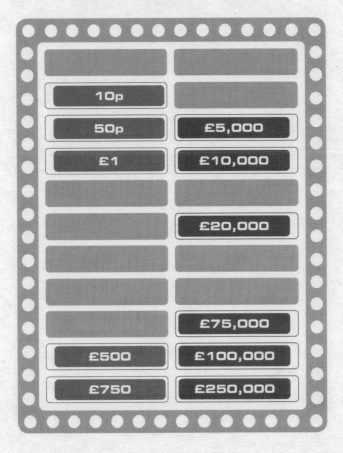

What do you think
The Banker's offer was?

....

151

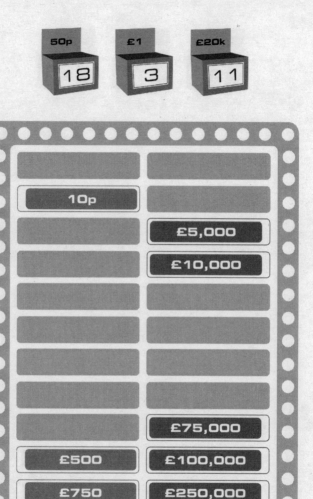

10p	
	£5,000
	£10,000
	£75,000
£500	£100,000
£750	£250,000

**What do you think
The Banker's offer was?**

....

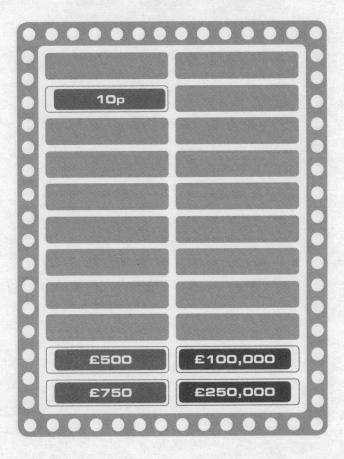

10p

£500 £100,000

£750 £250,000

**What do you think
The Banker's offer was?**

....

10p	£500	£100k
19	6	7

£750

£250,000

What do you think
The Banker's offer was?

✓ DEAL

....

154

TOTALISER

ROUND	BANKER'S OFFER
01	£2,300
02	
03	
04	
05	
06	
TOTAL	

What total do you think The Banker's offers in this game (including the first round) add up to?

A. £67,300   **B.** £227,900   **C.** £15,000

GAME 06
CONTESTANT'S BOX

10

1p	£1k	£10k	£50k	£250k
8	12	3	16	18

10p	£3,000
50p	£5,000
£1	
£5	£15,000
£10	£20,000
£50	£35,000
£100	
£250	£75,000
£500	£100,000
£750	

BANKER'S OFFER
£1,000

X NO DEAL

156

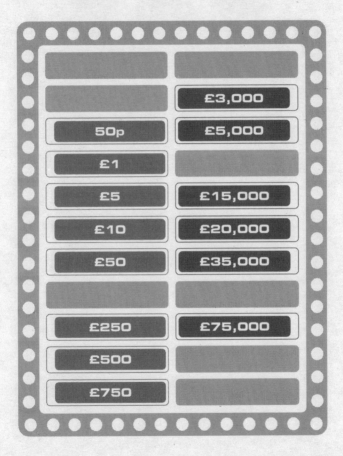

	£3,000
50p	£5,000
£1	
£5	£15,000
£10	£20,000
£50	£35,000
£250	£75,000
£500	
£750	

**What do you think
The Banker's offer was?**

....

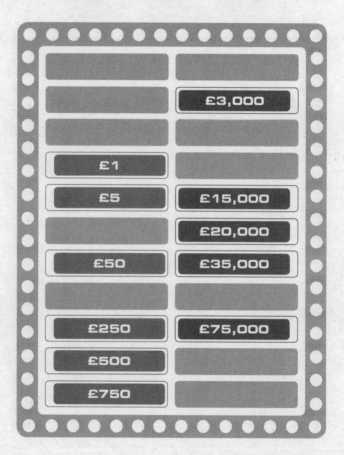

What do you think
The Banker's offer was?

	£3,000
£1	
£5	£15,000
	£20,000
£250	£75,000
£500	

**What do you think
The Banker's offer was?**

....

159

£1 — 17
£15k — 7
£20k — 15

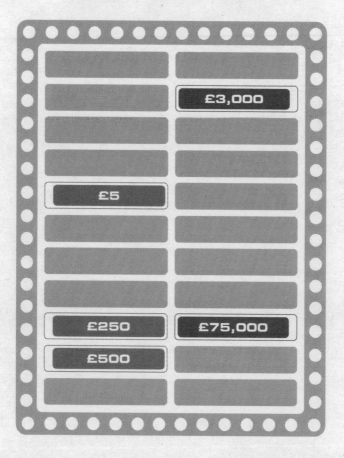

£3,000

£5

£250   £75,000

£500

What do you think
The Banker's offer was?

....

DEAL

160

TOTALISER

ROUND	BANKER'S OFFER
01	£1,000
02	
03	
04	
05	
TOTAL	

What total do you think The Banker's offers in this game (including the first round) add up to?

A. £30,900   **B.** £142,000   **C.** £93,200

GAME 07

CONTESTANT'S BOX 6

£50 — 2
£100 — 5
£250 — 9
£15k — 12
£100k — 18

1p	£1,000
10p	£3,000
50p	£5,000
£1	£10,000
£5	
£10	£20,000
	£35,000
	£50,000
	£75,000
£500	
£750	£250,000

BANKER'S OFFER
£900

X **NO DEAL**

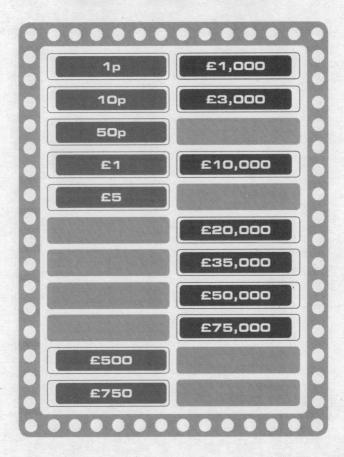

1p	£1,000
10p	£3,000
50p	
£1	£10,000
£5	
	£20,000
	£35,000
	£50,000
	£75,000
£500	
£750	

What do you think The Banker's offer was?

NO DEAL

....

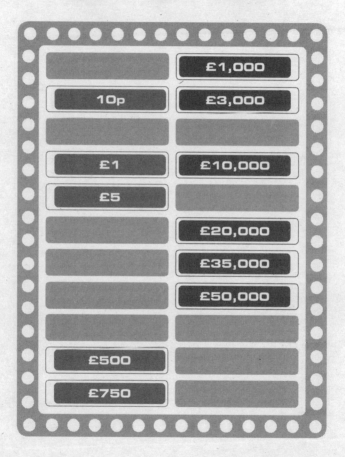

	£1,000
10p	£3,000
£1	£10,000
£5	
	£20,000
	£35,000
	£50,000
£500	
£750	

What do you think The Banker's offer was?

....

164

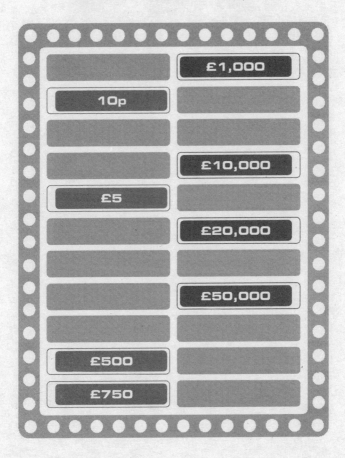

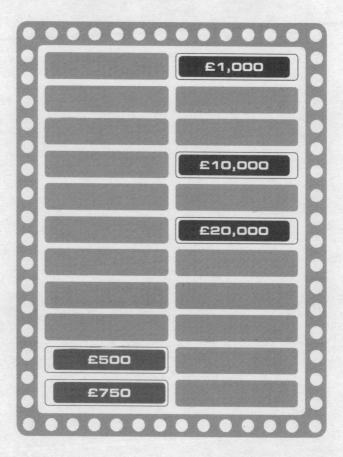

£1,000

£10,000

£20,000

£500

£750

**What do you think
The Banker's offer was?**

....

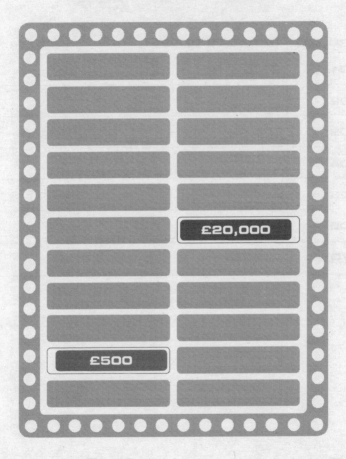

£20,000

£500

What do you think
The Banker's offer was?

....

TOTALISER

ROUND	BANKER'S OFFER
01	£900
02	
03	
04	
05	
06	
TOTAL	

What total do you think The Banker's offers in this game (including the first round) **add up to?**

A. £85,000   **B.** £31,800   **C.** £123,400

50p	£50	£250	£20k	£250k
16	9	3	6	1

1p	£1,000
10p	£3,000
	£5,000
£1	£10,000
£5	£15,000
£10	
	£35,000
£100	£50,000
	£75,000
£500	£100,000
£750	

BANKER'S OFFER
£1,400

X **NO DEAL**

1p	£1,000
10p	£3,000
	£10,000
£5	£15,000
£10	
	£35,000
£100	
	£75,000
£500	£100,000
£750	

**What do you think
The Banker's offer was?**

....

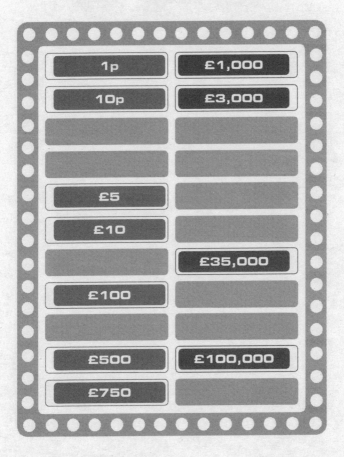

What do you think
The Banker's offer was?

....

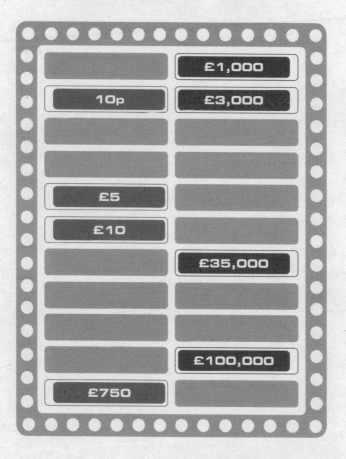

	£1,000
10p	£3,000
£5	
£10	
	£35,000
	£100,000
£750	

**What do you think
The Banker's offer was?**

....

172

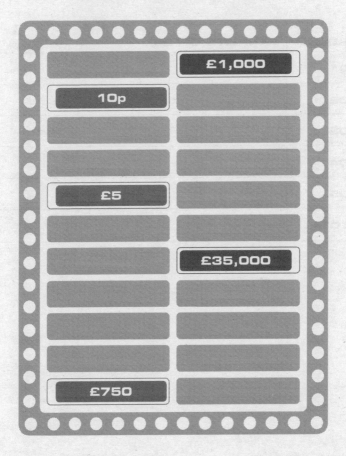

What do you think The Banker's offer was?

....

TOTALISER

ROUND	BANKER'S OFFER
01	£1,400
02	
03	
04	
05	
TOTAL	

What total do you think The Banker's offers in this game (including the first round) add up to?

A. £80,000   **B.** £58,400   **C.** £10,900

50p	£750	£1k	£3k	£5k
3	21	2	11	4

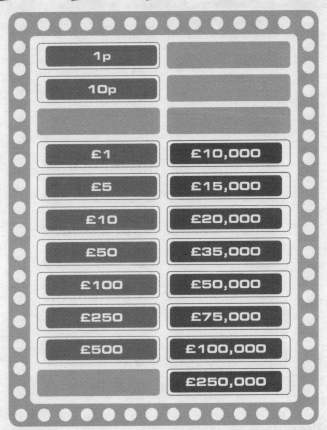

1p	
10p	
£1	£10,000
£5	£15,000
£10	£20,000
£50	£35,000
£100	£50,000
£250	£75,000
£500	£100,000
	£250,000

BANKER'S OFFER
£2,100

X **NO DEAL**

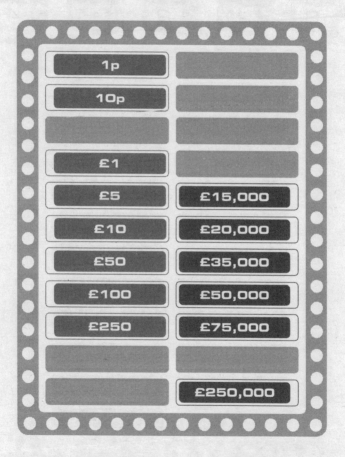

1p	
10p	
£1	
£5	£15,000
£10	£20,000
£50	£35,000
£100	£50,000
£250	£75,000
	£250,000

**What do you think
The Banker's offer was?**

....

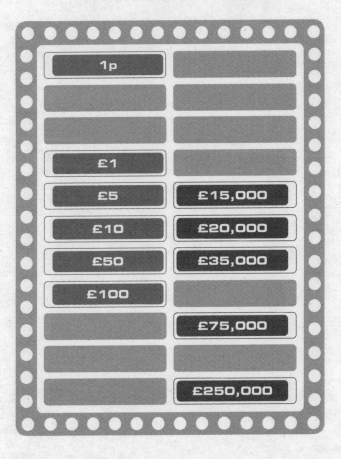

What do you think
The Banker's offer was?

....

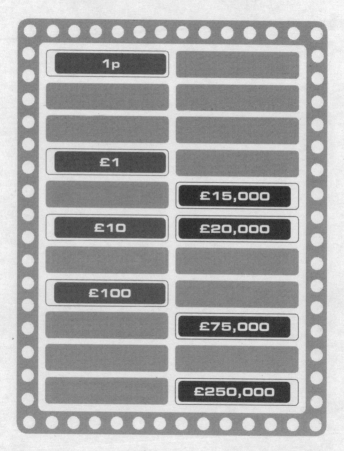

What do you think The Banker's offer was?

....

178

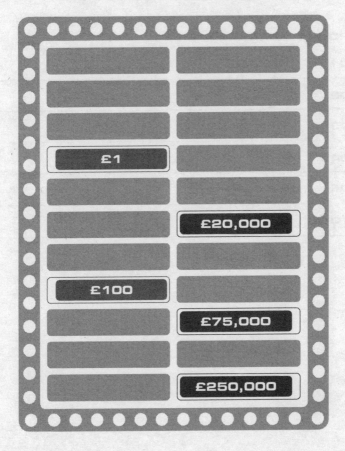

£1

£20,000

£100

£75,000

£250,000

What do you think
The Banker's offer was?

....

TOTALISER

ROUND	BANKER'S OFFER
01	£2,100
02	
03	
04	
05	
TOTAL	

What total do you think The Banker's offers in this game (including the first round) add up to?

A. £43,900   **B.** £13,900   **C.** £111,600

GAME 10

CONTESTANT'S BOX `14`

£1	£1k	£5k	£100k	£250k
6	5	4	3	19

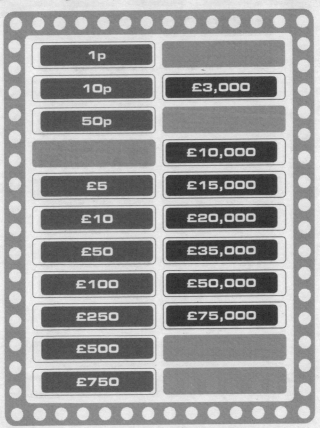

1p	
10p	£3,000
50p	
	£10,000
£5	£15,000
£10	£20,000
£50	£35,000
£100	£50,000
£250	£75,000
£500	
£750	

BANKER'S OFFER £500

X NO DEAL

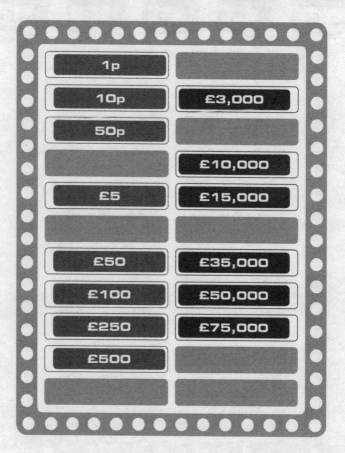

1p	
10p	£3,000
50p	
	£10,000
£5	£15,000
£50	£35,000
£100	£50,000
£250	£75,000
£500	

**What do you think
The Banker's offer was?**

....

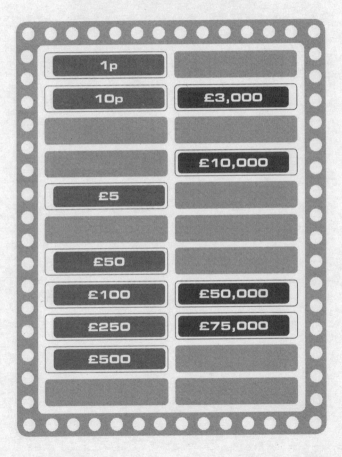

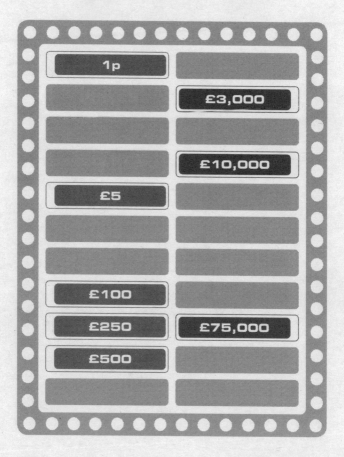

What do you think
The Banker's offer was?

....

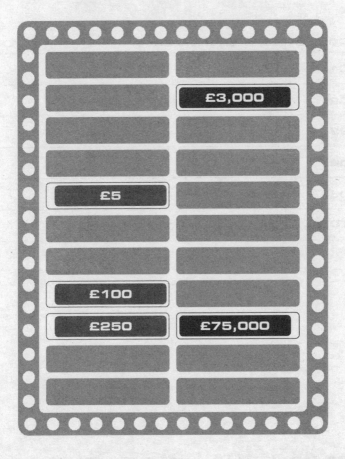

£3,000

£5

£100

£250   £75,000

What do you think The Banker's offer was?

....

TOTALISER

ROUND	BANKER'S OFFER
01	£500
02	
03	
04	
05	
TOTAL	

What total do you think The Banker's offers in this game (including the first round) add up to?

A. £4,000   **B.** £73,000   **C.** £10,500

ANSWERS
TOTALISER
BEGINNER

Fill in your answers here, then check on page 388 to see how many you got correct.

GAME 01	01	02	03	04	05
OFFER	£2,900				

What do all The Banker's offers in this game (including the first round) add up to?

A. £73,400   **B.** £16,500   **C.** £198,400

GAME 02	01	02	03	04	05
OFFER	£3,900				

What do all The Banker's offers in this game (including the first round) add up to?

A. £53,800   **B.** £14,000   **C.** £99,700

GAME 03	01	02	03	04	05	06
OFFER	£6,900					

What do all The Banker's offers in this game (including the first round) add up to?

A. £24,200   **B.** £123,000   **C.** £60,900

GAME 04	01	02	03	04	05
OFFER	£700				

What do all The Banker's offers in this game (including the first round) add up to?

A. £98,900   **B.** £1,300   **C.** £37,900

GAME 05	01	02	03	04	05	06
OFFER	£2,300					

What do all The Banker's offers in this game (including the first round) add up to?

A. £67,300   **B.** £227,900   **C.** £15,000

GAME 06	01	02	03	04	05
OFFER	£1,000				

**What do all The Banker's offers in this game
(including the first round) add up to?**

A. £30,900   **B.** £142,000   **C.** £93,200

GAME 07	01	02	03	04	05	06
OFFER	£900					

**What do all The Banker's offers in this game
(including the first round) add up to?**

A. £85,000   **B.** £31,800   **C.** £123,400

GAME 08	01	02	03	04	05
OFFER	£1,400				

**What do all The Banker's offers in this game
(including the first round) add up to?**

A. £80,000   **B.** £58,400   **C.** £10,900

GAME 09	01	02	03	04	05
OFFER	£2,100				

**What do all The Banker's offers in this game
(including the first round) add up to?**

A. £43,900   **B.** £13,900   **C.** £111,600

GAME 10	01	02	03	04	05
OFFER	£500				

**What do all The Banker's offers in this game
(including the first round) add up to?**

A. £4,000   **B.** £73,000   **C.** £10,500

CHAPTER 05
TOTALISER:
EXPERT

How did you get on? Because in this chapter it just got harder. A lot harder. This is the expert version of the last game, the Totaliser, and you are going to need every scrap of cunning, every ounce of brain power and every little piece of information you've put together about The Banker and how he operates.

Remember, he did not want the contestants to win, and he doesn't want you to win either. He likes his money, he likes it very much. And he likes to win, even if it's only a few pennies. He wants to humiliate you. Don't let him. Hold your nerve. He's only human, though you wouldn't always know it. He may be ruthless and merciless and very, very cunning, but he's not infallible. No one is.

Before you start to play this round, go back in your head over everything you've learned so far. Everything put together will lead you towards the answer to the question: 'what's he going to do next?' It's ringing, go get him!

GAME 01
CONTESTANT'S BOX | 9

10p — 11	
£50 — 17	
£35k — 18	
£75k — 3	
£100k — 22	

1p	£1,000
	£3,000
50p	£5,000
£1	£10,000
£5	£15,000
£10	£20,000
£100	£50,000
£250	
£500	
£750	£250,000

BANKER'S OFFER
£1,000

X NO DEAL

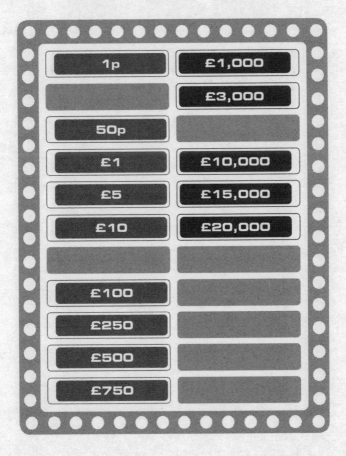

1p	£1,000
	£3,000
50p	
£1	£10,000
£5	£15,000
£10	£20,000
£100	
£250	
£500	
£750	

**What do you think
The Banker's offer was?**

....

195

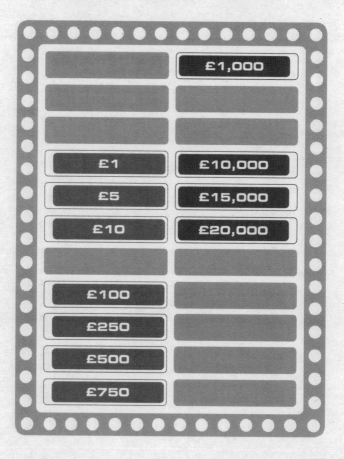

What do you think
The Banker's offer was?

....

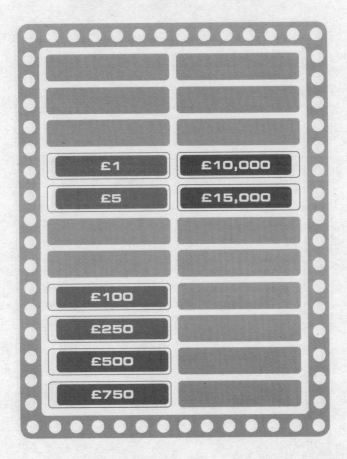

£1	£10,000
£5	£15,000
£100	
£250	
£500	
£750	

**What do you think
The Banker's offer was?**

....

197

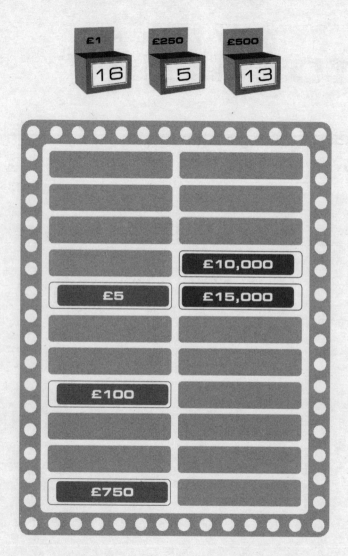

	£10,000
£5	£15,000
£100	
£750	

£1 — 16
£250 — 5
£500 — 13

What do you think The Banker's offer was?

 DEAL

TOTALISER

ROUND	BANKER'S OFFER
01	£1,000
02	
03	
04	
05	
TOTAL	

What total do you think The Banker's offer in this game (including the first round) add up to?

A. £14,600   **B.** £7,700   **C.** £15,300

50p	£50	£750	£15k	£50k
16	22	1	2	3

1p	£1,000
10p	£3,000
	£5,000
£1	£10,000
£5	
£10	£20,000
	£35,000
£100	
£250	£75,000
£500	£100,000
	£250,000

BANKER'S OFFER
£1,400

X **NO DEAL**

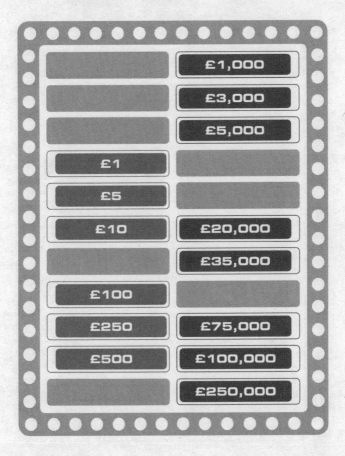

	£1,000
	£3,000
	£5,000
£1	
£5	
£10	£20,000
	£35,000
£100	
£250	£75,000
£500	£100,000
	£250,000

**What do you think
The Banker's offer was?**

....

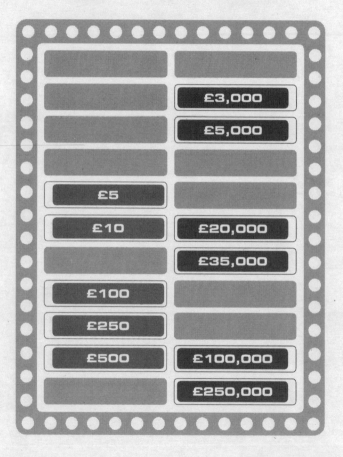

	£3,000
	£5,000
£5	
£10	£20,000
	£35,000
£100	
£250	
£500	£100,000
	£250,000

**What do you think
The Banker's offer was?**

....

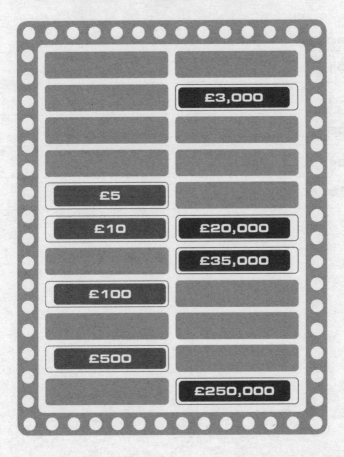

£3,000

£5

£10   £20,000

£35,000

£100

£500

£250,000

What do you think
The Banker's offer was?

 DEAL

....

TOTALISER

ROUND	BANKER'S OFFER
01	£1,400
02	
03	
04	
TOTAL	

What total do you think The Banker's offers in this game (including the first round) add up to?

A. £92,300   **B.** £32,300   **C.** £78,400

GAME 03

CONTESTANT'S BOX

13

£5	£500	£750	£3k	£15k
1	19	2	12	6

1p	£1,000
10p	
50p	£5,000
£1	£10,000
£10	£20,000
£50	£35,000
£100	£50,000
£250	£75,000
	£100,000
	£250,000

BANKER'S OFFER
£9,000

X NO DEAL

1p	
10p	
50p	£5,000
£1	£10,000
£10	£20,000
£50	
£100	£50,000
£250	£75,000
	£100,000

**What do you think
The Banker's offer was?**

....

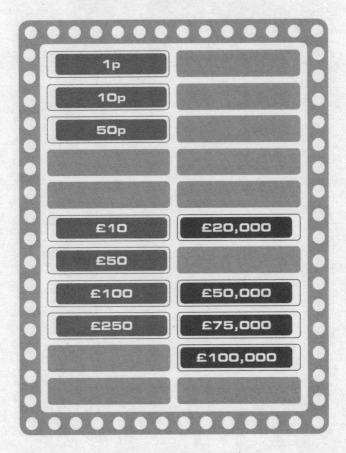

What do you think
The Banker's offer was?

X NO DEAL

....

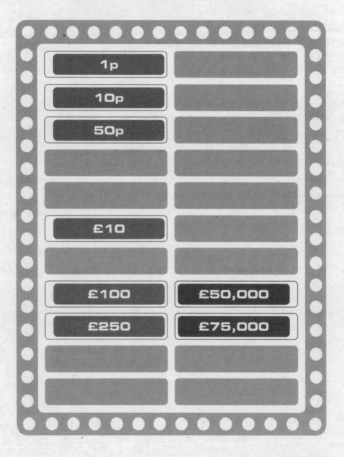

1p	
10p	
50p	
£10	
£100	£50,000
£250	£75,000

**What do you think
The Banker's offer was?**

....

208

TOTALISER

ROUND	BANKER'S OFFER
01	£9,000
02	
03	
04	
TOTAL	

What total do you think The Banker's offers in this game (including the first round) add up to?

A. £21,100   **B.** £89,000   **C.** £6,900

GAME 04

CONTESTANT'S BOX

3

10p	£1	£750	£1k	£75k
8	17	4	6	1

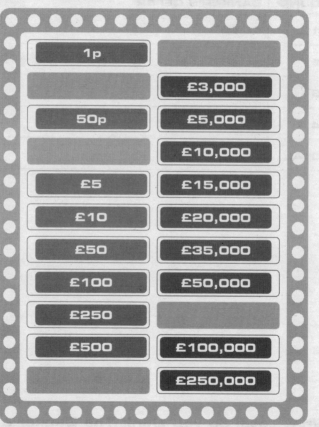

1p	
	£3,000
50p	£5,000
	£10,000
£5	£15,000
£10	£20,000
£50	£35,000
£100	£50,000
£250	
£500	£100,000
	£250,000

BANKER'S OFFER
£1,100

X NO DEAL

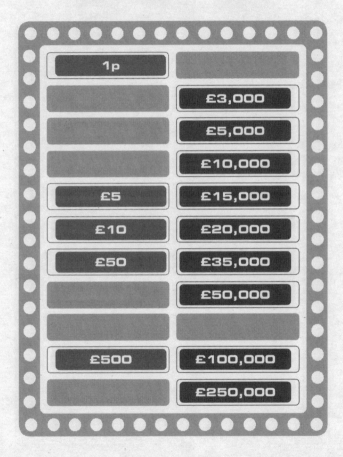

1p	
	£3,000
	£5,000
	£10,000
£5	£15,000
£10	£20,000
£50	£35,000
	£50,000
£500	£100,000
	£250,000

**What do you think
The Banker's offer was?**

....

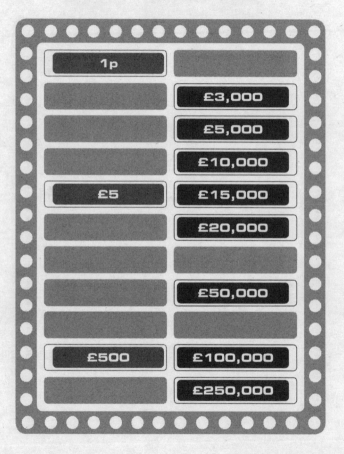

What do you think
The Banker's offer was?

....

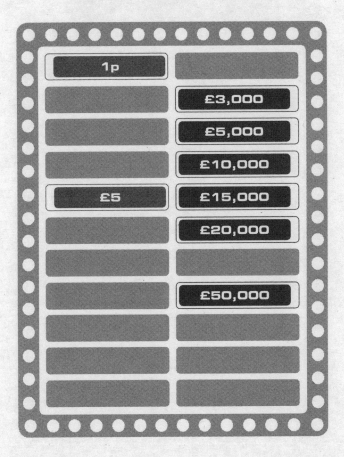

1p	
	£3,000
	£5,000
	£10,000
£5	£15,000
	£20,000
	£50,000

What do you think The Banker's offer was?

....

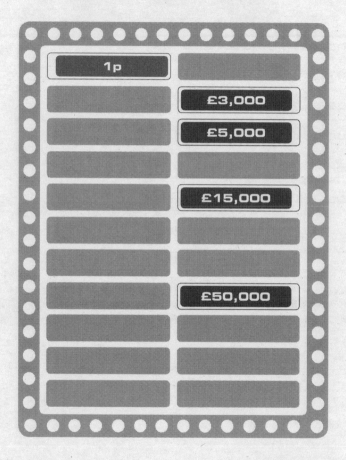

TOTALISER

ROUND	BANKER'S OFFER
01	£1,100
02	
03	
04	
05	
TOTAL	

What total do you think The Banker's offers in this game (including the first round) add up to?

A. £35,800   **B.** £21,500   **C.** £72,400

10p	£100	£750	£1k	£20k
6	13	10	4	5

1p	
	£3,000
50p	£5,000
£1	£10,000
£5	£15,000
£10	
£50	£35,000
	£50,000
£250	£75,000
£500	£100,000
	£250,000

BANKER'S OFFER
£3,200

X **NO DEAL**

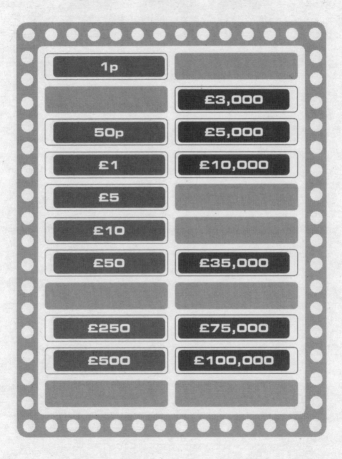

What do you think
The Banker's offer was?

....

217

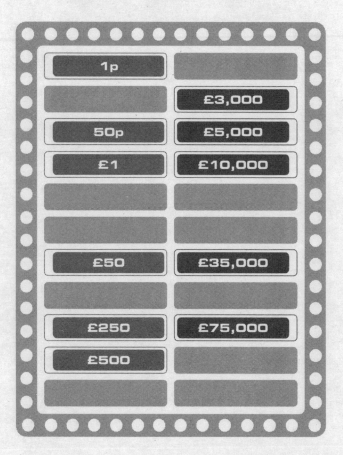

1p	
	£3,000
50p	£5,000
£1	£10,000
£50	£35,000
£250	£75,000
£500	

**What do you think
The Banker's offer was?**

....

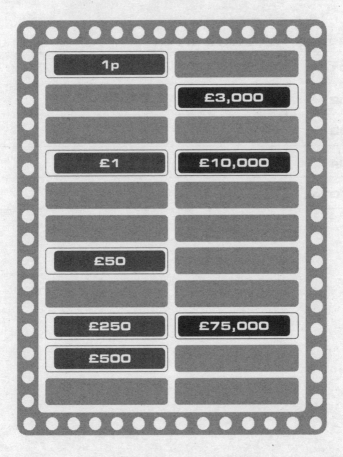

1p	
	£3,000
£1	£10,000
£50	
£250	£75,000
£500	

**What do you think
The Banker's offer was?**

....

219

TOTALISER

ROUND	BANKER'S OFFER
01	£3,200
02	
03	
04	
TOTAL	

What total do you think The Banker's offers in this game (including the first round) add up to?

A. £42,000   **B.** £13,800   **C.** £9,300

1p	£100	£5k	£15k	£250k
16	18	8	9	20

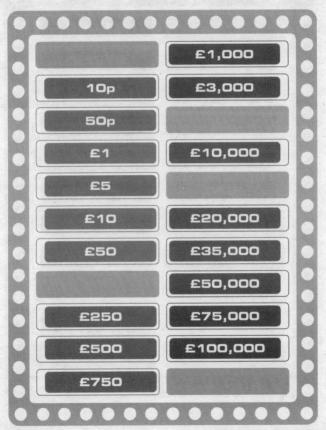

	£1,000
10p	£3,000
50p	
£1	£10,000
£5	
£10	£20,000
£50	£35,000
	£50,000
£250	£75,000
£500	£100,000
£750	

BANKER'S OFFER
£800

X NO DEAL

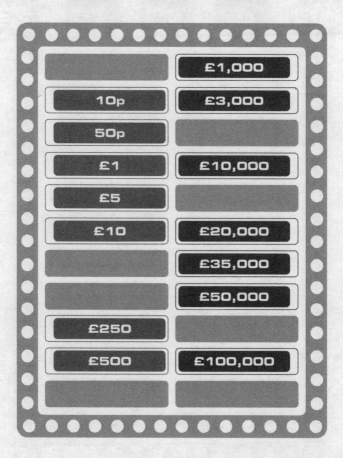

What do you think The Banker's offer was?

....

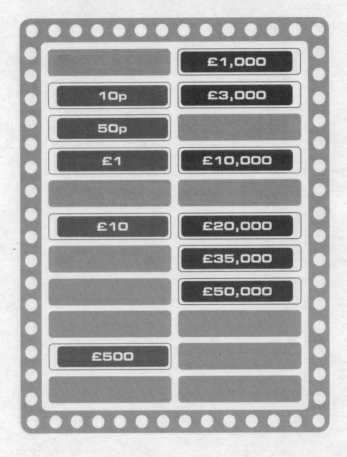

	£1,000
10p	£3,000
50p	
£1	£10,000
£10	£20,000
	£35,000
	£50,000
£500	

**What do you think
The Banker's offer was?**

....

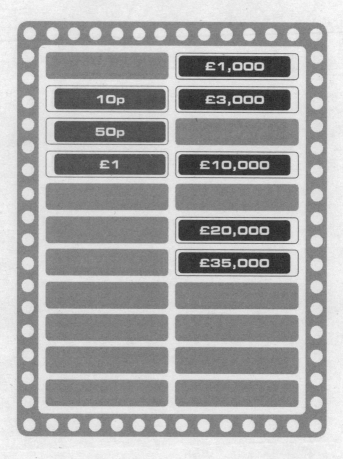

What do you think The Banker's offer was?

....

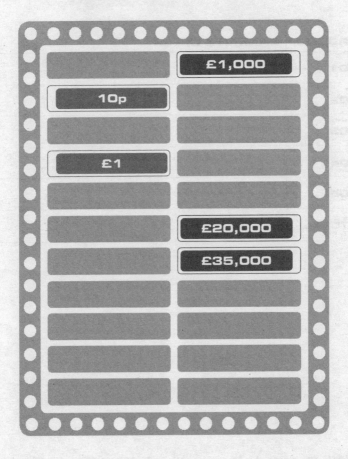

What do you think
The Banker's offer was?

....

TOTALISER

ROUND	BANKER'S OFFER
01	£800
02	
03	
04	
05	
TOTAL	

What total do you think The Banker's offers in this game (including the first round) add up to?

A. £4,000   **B.** £16,700   **C.** £12,400

1p	£250	£750	£50k	£100k
9	11	5	3	21

	£1,000
10p	£3,000
50p	£5,000
£1	£10,000
£5	£15,000
£10	£20,000
£50	£35,000
£100	
	£75,000
£500	
	£250,000

BANKER'S OFFER
£1,300

X **NO DEAL**

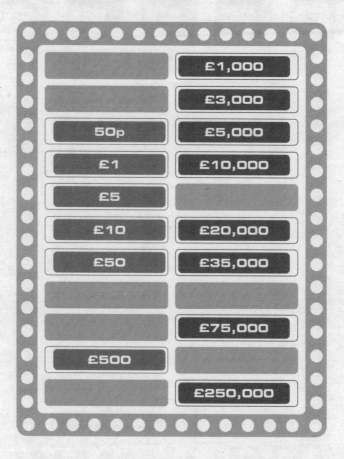

	£1,000
	£3,000
50p	£5,000
£1	£10,000
£5	
£10	£20,000
£50	£35,000
	£75,000
£500	
	£250,000

**What do you think
The Banker's offer was?**

....

228

	£1,000
	£3,000
50p	£5,000
£1	£10,000
£5	
£10	£20,000
£50	£35,000

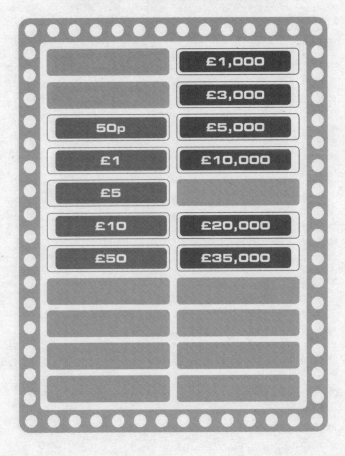

What do you think The Banker's offer was?

....

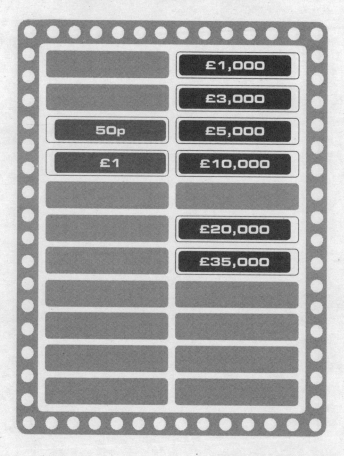

What do you think
The Banker's offer was?

....

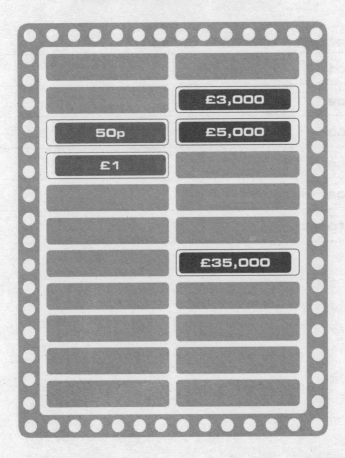

	£3,000
50p	£5,000
£1	
	£35,000

What do you think The Banker's offer was?

....

TOTALISER

ROUND	BANKER'S OFFER
01	£1,300
02	
03	
04	
05	
TOTAL	

What total do you think The Banker's offers in this game (including the first round) add up to?

A. £16,300   **B.** £28,400   **C.** £48,400

£1k	£10k	£75k	£100k	£250k
2	1	4	13	20

1p	
10p	£3,000
50p	£5,000
£1	
£5	£15,000
£10	£20,000
£50	£35,000
£100	£50,000
£250	
£500	
£750	

BANKER'S OFFER
£300

X NO DEAL

50p	£10	£250
21	12	17

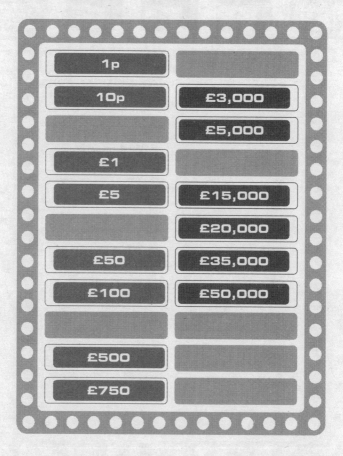

1p	
10p	£3,000
	£5,000
£1	
£5	£15,000
	£20,000
£50	£35,000
£100	£50,000
£500	
£750	

**What do you think
The Banker's offer was?**

....

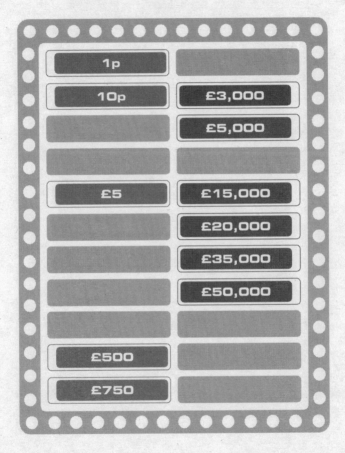

1p	
10p	£3,000
	£5,000
£5	£15,000
	£20,000
	£35,000
	£50,000
£500	
£750	

What do you think
The Banker's offer was?

....

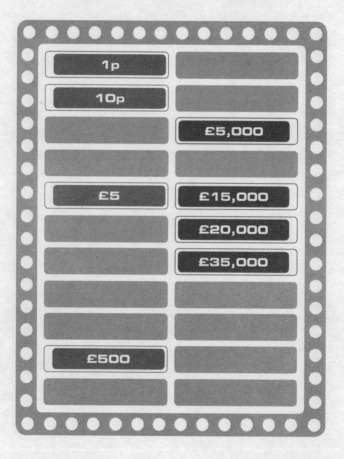

1p	
10p	
	£5,000
£5	£15,000
	£20,000
	£35,000
£500	

What do you think
The Banker's offer was?

....

236

1p	
	£15,000
	£20,000
	£35,000
£500	

**What do you think
The Banker's offer was?**

DEAL

....

237

TOTALISER

ROUND	BANKER'S OFFER
01	£300
02	
03	
04	
05	
TOTAL	

What total do you think The Banker's offers in this game (including the first round) add up to?

A. £67,000   **B.** £15,500   **C.** £53,000

ANSWERS

TOTALISER
EXPERT

Fill in your answers here, then check on page 389 to see how many you got correct.

GAME 01	01	02	03	04	05
OFFER	£1,000				

What do all The Banker's offers in this game (including the first round) add up to?

A. £14,600   **B.** £7,700   **C.** £15,300

GAME 02	01	02	03	04
OFFER	£1,400			

What do all The Banker's offers in this game (including the first round) add up to?

A. £92,300   **B.** £32,300   **C.** £78,400

GAME 03	01	02	03	04
OFFER	£9,000			

What do all The Banker's offers in this game (including the first round) add up to?

A. £21,100   **B.** £89,000   **C.** £6,900

GAME 04	01	02	03	04	05
OFFER	£1,100				

What do all The Banker's offers in this game (including the first round) add up to?

A. £35,800   **B.** £21,500   **C.** £72,400

GAME 05	01	02	03	04
OFFER	£3,200			

What do all The Banker's offers in this game (including the first round) add up to?

A. £42,000   **B.** £13,800   **C.** £9,300

GAME 06	01	02	03	04	05
OFFER	£800				

What do all The Banker's offers in this game (including the first round) add up to?

A. £4000   **B.** £16,700   **C.** £12,400

GAME 07	01	02	03	04	05
OFFER	£1,300				

What do all The Banker's offers in this game (including the first round) add up to?

A. £16,300   **B.** £28,400   **C.** £48,400

GAME 08	01	02	03	04	05
OFFER	£300				

What do all The Banker's offers in this game (including the first round) add up to?

A. £67,000   **B.** £15,500   **C.** £53,000

CHAPTER 06
BEAT THE BANKER:
BEGINNER

It's been quite a journey, but you're nearly there now. I hope you're ready, because this is where you go head to head with The Banker. The previous five chapters have all led up to this point. This is the game we call Beat The Banker. We'll start you off on a slightly easier version which should prepare you for the ultimate test in the next, and last, chapter.

This is the game that puts you in the hot seat, alone. You will see the first few rounds, the offers made by The Banker, and the boxes that were opened afterwards. Then The Banker will make an offer and you have to make a decision. The ultimate decision. Deal Or No Deal. Will you win more money if you carry on or is this offer the highest The Banker will go? Then you turn to the answers section at the end of the book and see if you were right or wrong.

Whether you have learned anything at all, whether you have got what it takes. You have got to keep your nerve. You should know how he works by now. Did he go higher? Or has he beaten you again? Don't let it get to you. Be cool.

Ready? Pick up the phone...

GAME 01
CONTESTANT'S BOX

1

50p 6	**£1** 21	**£250** 20	**£75k** 7	**£100k** 19

1p	£1,000
10p	£3,000
	£5,000
	£10,000
£5	£15,000
£10	£20,000
£50	£35,000
£100	£50,000
£500	
£750	£250,000

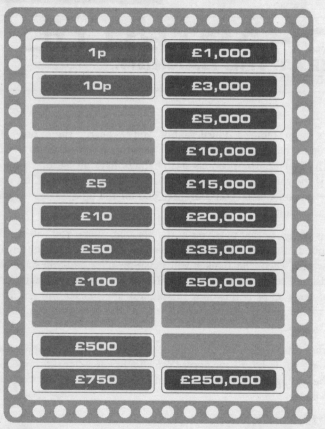

BANKER'S OFFER
£600

X NO DEAL

10p	£10	£500
16	22	17

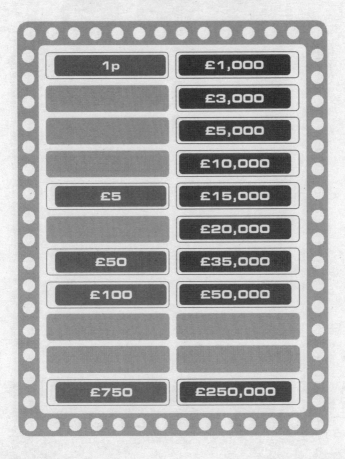

1p	£1,000
	£3,000
	£5,000
	£10,000
£5	£15,000
	£20,000
£50	£35,000
£100	£50,000
£750	£250,000

BANKER'S OFFER £6,000

X **NO DEAL**

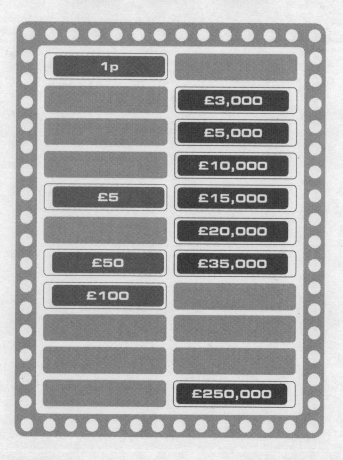

1p	
	£3,000
	£5,000
	£10,000
£5	£15,000
	£20,000
£50	£35,000
£100	
	£250,000

BANKER'S OFFER

£7,500

Tick a box and turn to
page 390 for the answer.

✓ DEAL

✓ NO DEAL

10p	£500	£3k	£20k	£250k
7	2	5	8	4

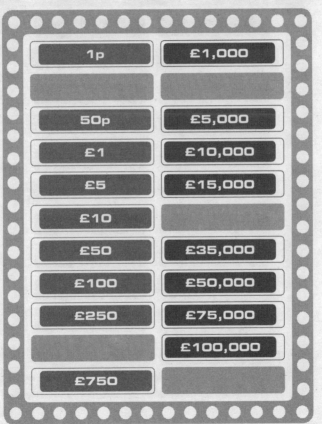

1p	£1,000
50p	£5,000
£1	£10,000
£5	£15,000
£10	
£50	£35,000
£100	£50,000
£250	£75,000
	£100,000
£750	

BANKER'S OFFER
£2,100

X NO DEAL

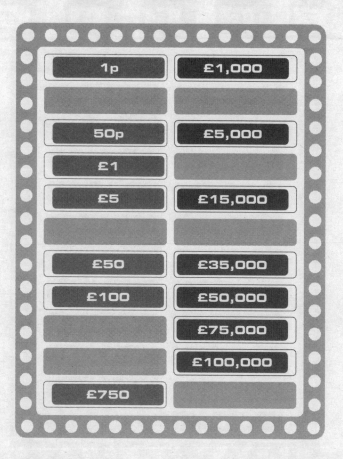

1p	£1,000
50p	£5,000
£1	
£5	£15,000
£50	£35,000
£100	£50,000
	£75,000
	£100,000
£750	

BANKER'S OFFER £5,600

X NO DEAL

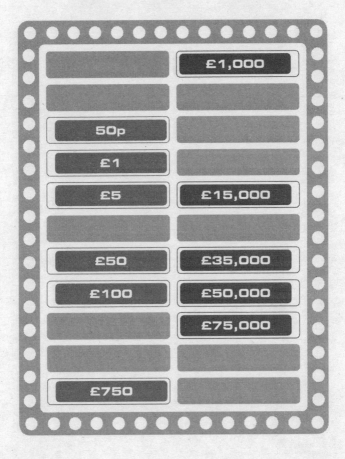

	£1,000
50p	
£1	
£5	£15,000
£50	£35,000
£100	£50,000
	£75,000
£750	

BANKER'S OFFER
£1,600

X NO DEAL

251

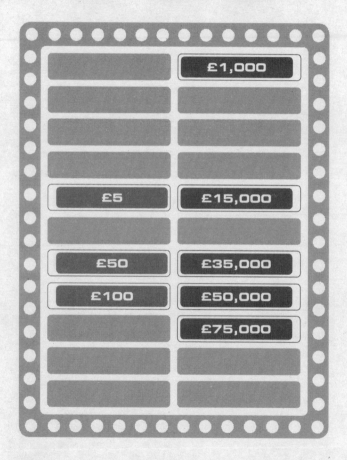

	£1,000
£5	£15,000
£50	£35,000
£100	£50,000
	£75,000

BANKER'S OFFER
£8,200
Tick a box and turn to
page 390 for the answer.

✓ DEAL

✓ NO DEAL

GAME 03

CONTESTANT'S BOX 20

1p	50p	£15k	£35k	£75k
3	11	18	6	16

	£1,000
10p	£3,000
	£5,000
£1	£10,000
£5	
£10	£20,000
£50	
£100	£50,000
£250	
£500	£100,000
£750	£250,000

BANKER'S OFFER
£1,800

X NO DEAL

£1	£50	£250k
13	5	19

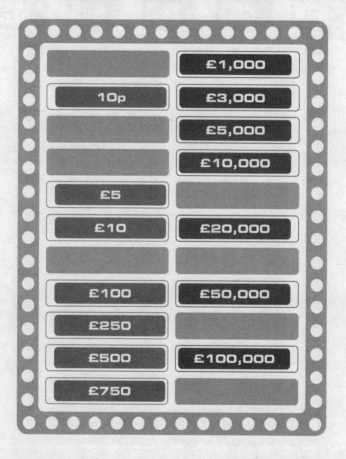

	£1,000
10p	£3,000
	£5,000
	£10,000
£5	
£10	£20,000
£100	£50,000
£250	
£500	£100,000
£750	

BANKER'S OFFER
£600

X NO DEAL

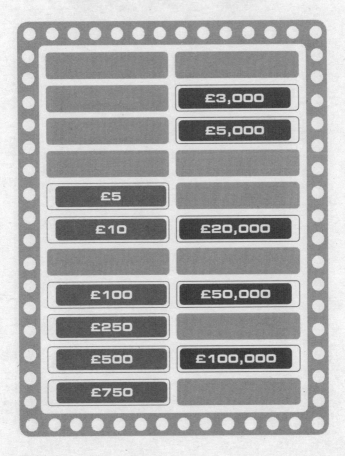

	£3,000
	£5,000
£5	
£10	£20,000
£100	£50,000
£250	
£500	£100,000
£750	

BANKER'S OFFER
£7,000

X NO DEAL

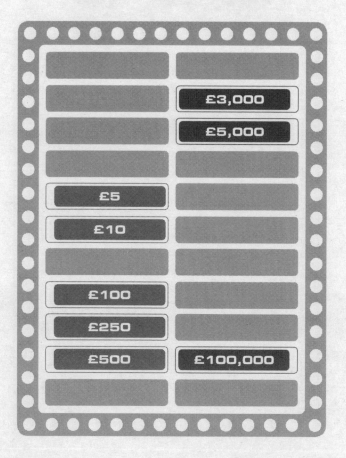

	£3,000
	£5,000
£5	
£10	
£100	
£250	
£500	£100,000

BANKER'S OFFER
£4,200

£5 £250 £3k
9   4   21

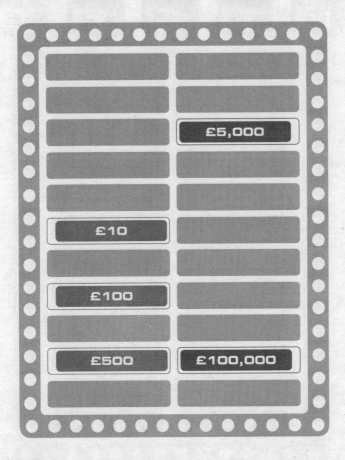

£5,000

£10

£100

£500   £100,000

BANKER'S OFFER
£13,000
Tick a box and turn to
page 391 for the answer.

✓ DEAL

✓ NO DEAL

1p	£10	£500	£1k	£50k
8	4	11	2	5

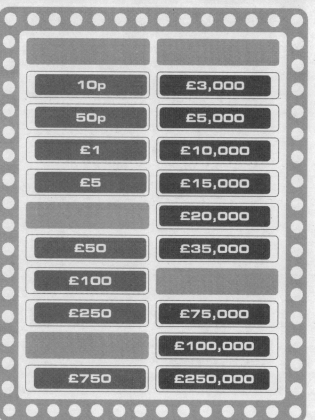

10p	£3,000
50p	£5,000
£1	£10,000
£5	£15,000
	£20,000
£50	£35,000
£100	
£250	£75,000
	£100,000
£750	£250,000

BANKER'S OFFER
£8,100

X NO DEAL

258

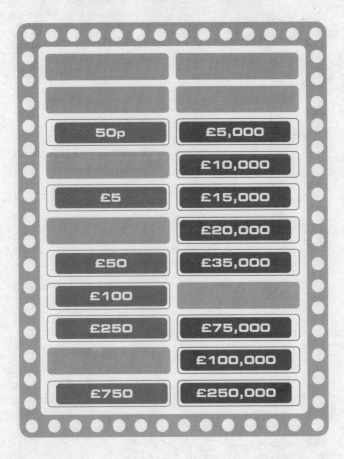

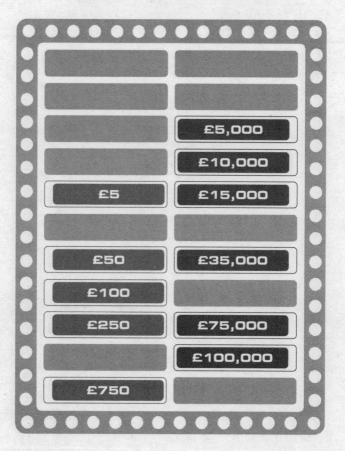

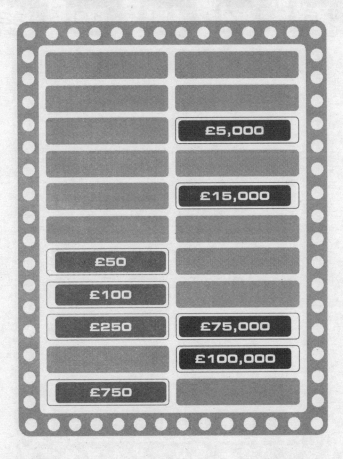

BANKER'S OFFER
£8,100
Tick a box and turn to
page 391 for the answer.

DEAL

NO DEAL

261

GAME 05
CONTESTANT'S BOX

15

£1	£50	£35k	£50k	£100k
5	7	11	10	22

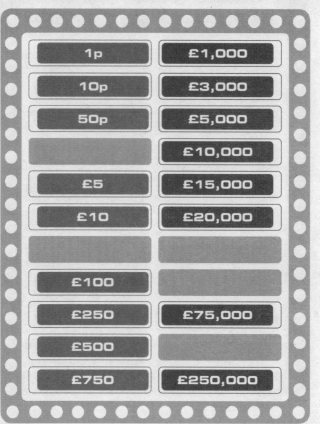

1p	£1,000
10p	£3,000
50p	£5,000
	£10,000
£5	£15,000
£10	£20,000
£100	
£250	£75,000
£500	
£750	£250,000

BANKER'S OFFER
£2,700

X NO DEAL

£100 — 9
£20k — 6
£75k — 2

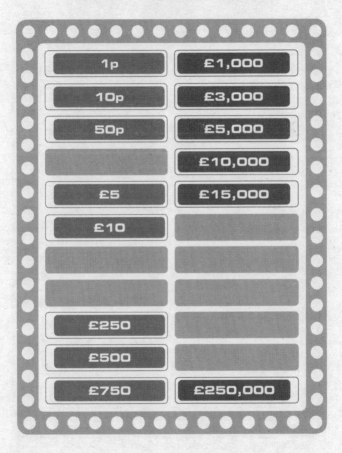

1p	£1,000
10p	£3,000
50p	£5,000
	£10,000
£5	£15,000
£10	
£250	
£500	
£750	£250,000

BANKER'S OFFER
£900

X NO DEAL

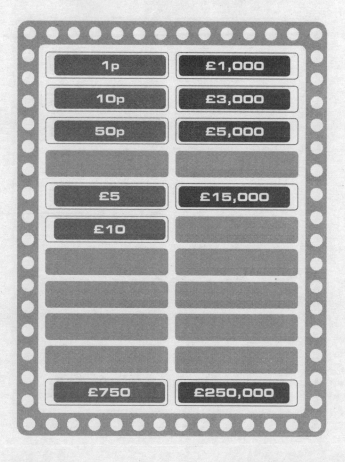

264

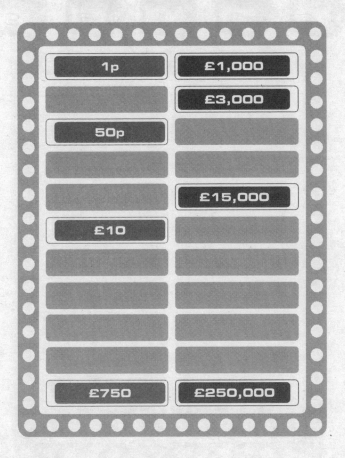

BANKER'S OFFER

£17,000

Tick a box and turn to
page 391 for the answer.

✓ DEAL

✓ NO DEAL

GAME 06
CONTESTANT'S BOX 10

10p 4	£100 3	£750 1	£50k 5	£250k 2

1p	£1,000
	£3,000
50p	£5,000
£1	£10,000
£5	£15,000
£10	£20,000
£50	£35,000
£250	£75,000
£500	£100,000

BANKER'S OFFER
£2,500

X NO DEAL

266

£250	£1k	£15k
9	8	18

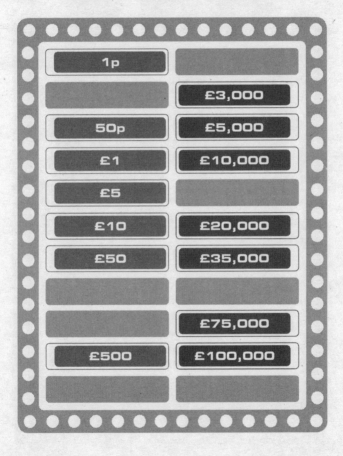

1p	
	£3,000
50p	£5,000
£1	£10,000
£5	
£10	£20,000
£50	£35,000
	£75,000
£500	£100,000

BANKER'S OFFER £5,300

X NO DEAL

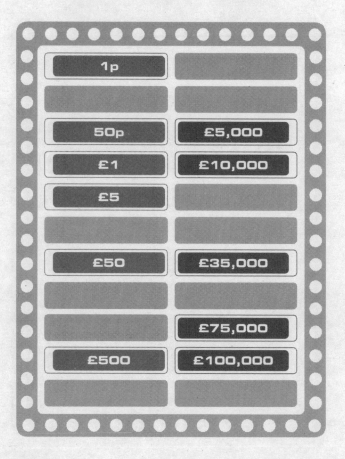

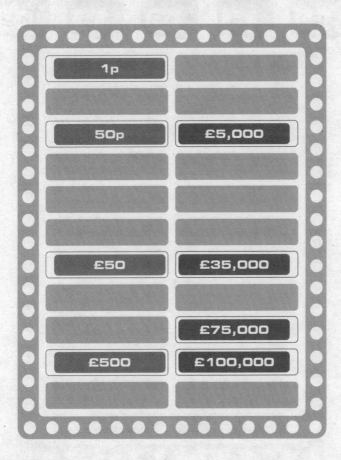

1p	
50p	£5,000
£50	£35,000
	£75,000
£500	£100,000

BANKER'S OFFER

£18,000

Tick a box and turn to
page 392 for the answer.

✓ DEAL

✓ NO DEAL

269

GAME 07
CONTESTANT'S BOX — 2

1p — 21	10p — 8	£50 — 19	£100 — 9	£75k — 12

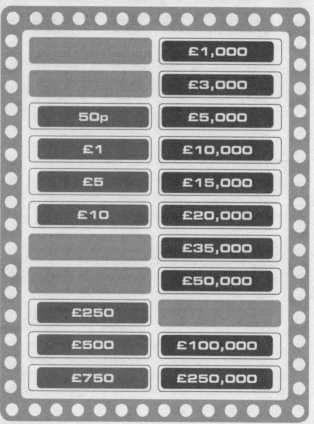

	£1,000
	£3,000
50p	£5,000
£1	£10,000
£5	£15,000
£10	£20,000
	£35,000
	£50,000
£250	
£500	£100,000
£750	£250,000

BANKER'S OFFER
£8,500

X NO DEAL

270

	50p	£250	£100k
	15	4	11

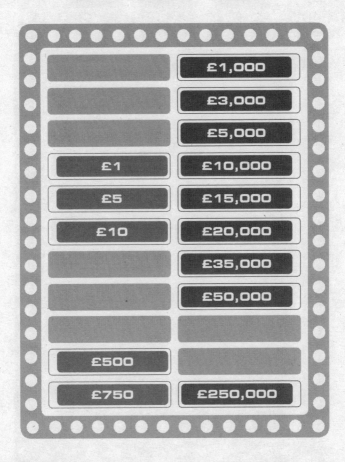

	£1,000
	£3,000
	£5,000
£1	£10,000
£5	£15,000
£10	£20,000
	£35,000
	£50,000
£500	
£750	£250,000

BANKER'S OFFER
£2,700

✗ NO DEAL

£500	£15k	£50k
17	14	13

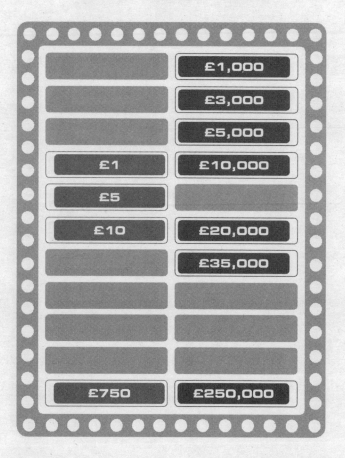

	£1,000
	£3,000
	£5,000
£1	£10,000
£5	
£10	£20,000
	£35,000
£750	£250,000

BANKER'S OFFER
£6,200

X **NO DEAL**

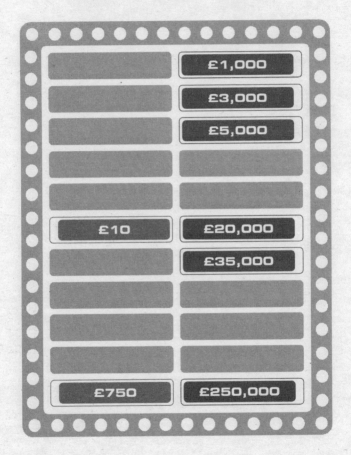

	£1,000
	£3,000
	£5,000
£10	£20,000
	£35,000
£750	£250,000

BANKER'S OFFER
£24,000

X NO DEAL

£1k 10   £5k 16   £35k 5

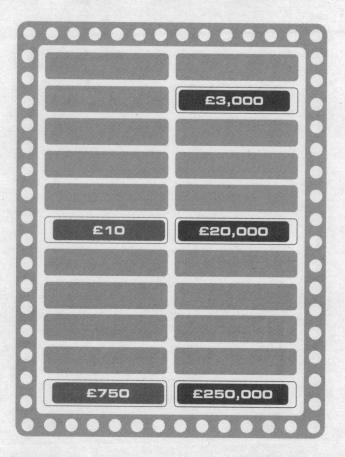

£3,000

£10   £20,000

£750   £250,000

GAME 08
CONTESTANT'S BOX

1

50p	£1	£1k	£3k	£20k
9	3	8	5	11

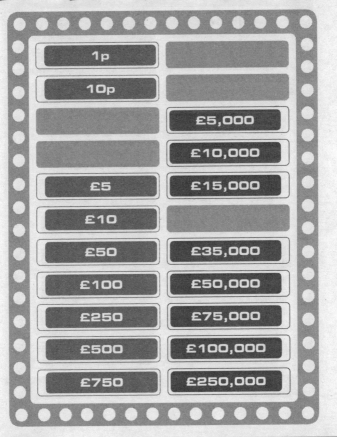

1p	
10p	
	£5,000
	£10,000
£5	£15,000
£10	
£50	£35,000
£100	£50,000
£250	£75,000
£500	£100,000
£750	£250,000

BANKER'S OFFER
£5,800

X NO DEAL

£100 18 £250 16 £100k 2

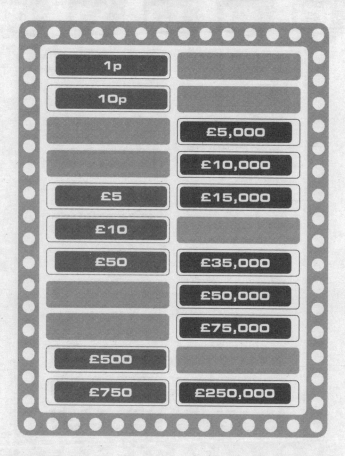

1p	
10p	
	£5,000
	£10,000
£5	£15,000
£10	
£50	£35,000
	£50,000
	£75,000
£500	
£750	£250,000

BANKER'S OFFER £3,100

X NO DEAL

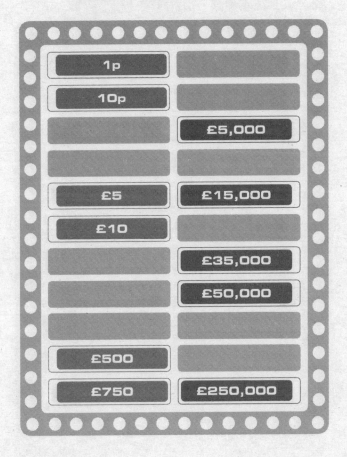

BANKER'S OFFER
£1,500

X NO DEAL

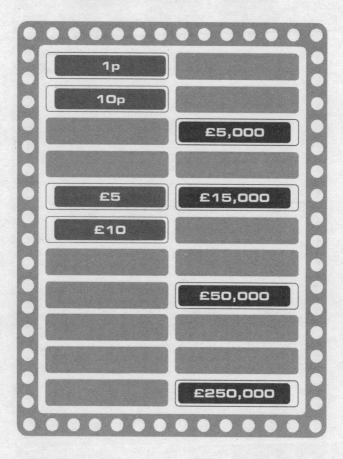

BANKER'S OFFER
£11,700
Tick a box and turn to page 392 for the answer.

DEAL

NO DEAL

GAME 09

CONTESTANT'S BOX 21

1p **14**	50p **3**	£1 **1**	£35k **9**	£250k **16**

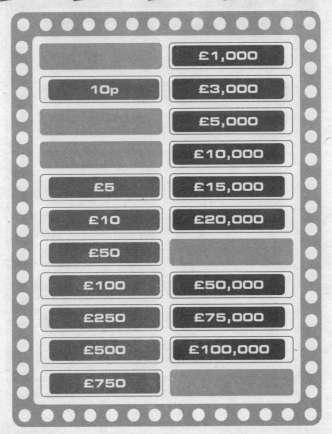

	£1,000
10p	£3,000
	£5,000
	£10,000
£5	£15,000
£10	£20,000
£50	
£100	£50,000
£250	£75,000
£500	£100,000
£750	

BANKER'S OFFER
£500

X NO DEAL

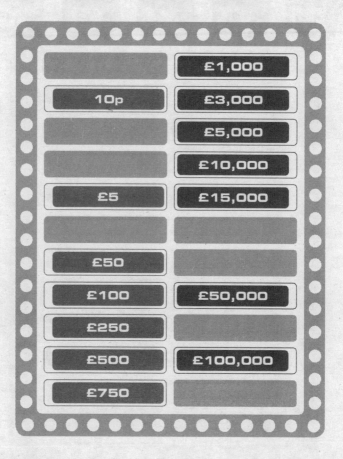

	£1,000
10p	£3,000
	£5,000
	£10,000
£5	£15,000
£50	
£100	£50,000
£250	
£500	£100,000
£750	

BANKER'S OFFER
£750

X NO DEAL

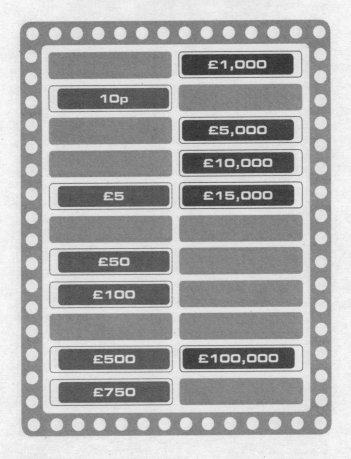

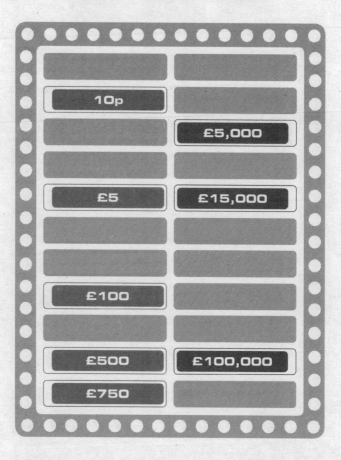

10p

£5,000

£5   £15,000

£100

£500   £100,000

£750

BANKER'S OFFER
£5,000

Tick a box and turn to
page 393 for the answer.

✓ DEAL

✓ NO DEAL

282

GAME 10

CONTESTANT'S BOX

13

£250 — 16	
£1k — 14	
£5k — 19	
£15k — 18	
£75k — 11	

1p	
10p	£3,000
50p	
£1	£10,000
£5	
£10	£20,000
£50	£35,000
£100	£50,000
£500	£100,000
£750	£250,000

BANKER'S OFFER
£2,200

X NO DEAL

1p	
50p	
£1	£10,000
£5	
£10	£20,000
£50	£35,000
£100	£50,000
£500	£100,000
£750	

 BANKER'S OFFER £600  NO DEAL

50p	
£1	£10,000
£5	
£10	£20,000
£50	£35,000
	£50,000
	£100,000
£750	

BANKER'S OFFER £14,000   ✕ NO DEAL

285

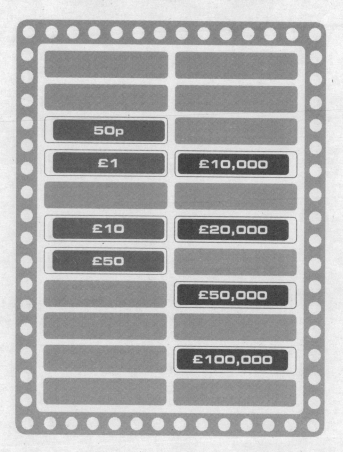

50p	
£1	£10,000
£10	£20,000
£50	
	£50,000
	£100,000

BANKER'S OFFER
£22,000
Tick a box and turn to
page 393 for the answer.

✓ DEAL

✓ NO DEAL

1p	£10	£100	£5k	£20k
2	22	12	11	20

	£1,000
10p	£3,000
50p	
£1	£10,000
£5	£15,000
£50	£35,000
	£50,000
£250	£75,000
£500	£100,000
£750	£250,000

BANKER'S OFFER
£6,300

X NO DEAL

	£1,000
10p	£3,000
50p	
£1	£10,000
£5	£15,000
£50	£35,000
	£75,000
	£100,000
£750	£250,000

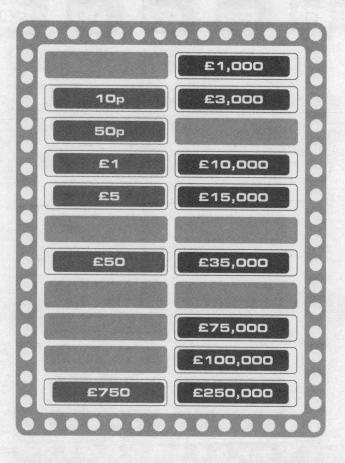

BANKER'S OFFER
£9,800

X NO DEAL

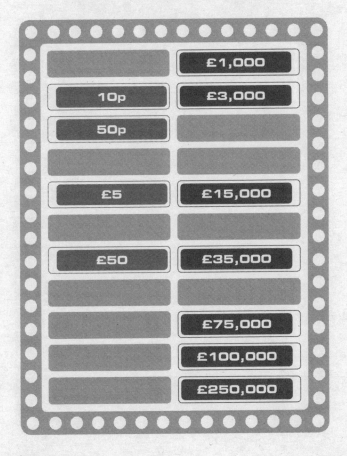

	£1,000
10p	£3,000
50p	
£5	£15,000
£50	£35,000
	£75,000
	£100,000
	£250,000

BANKER'S OFFER
£20,000

X NO DEAL

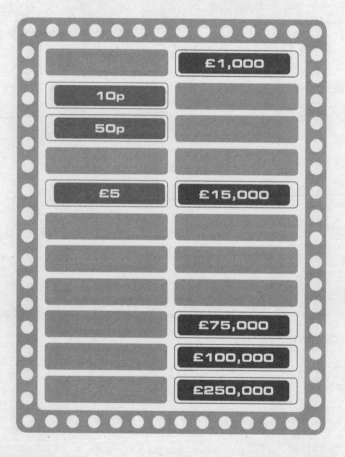

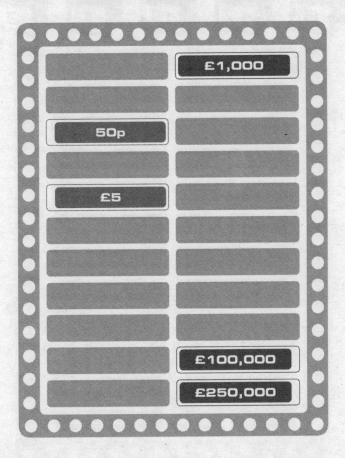

£1,000

50p

£5

£100,000

£250,000

BANKER'S OFFER
£55,000
Tick a box and turn to page 393 for the answer.

✓ DEAL

✓ NO DEAL

GAME 12
CONTESTANT'S BOX

15

£100	£250	£750	£50k	£75k
6	17	11	1	3

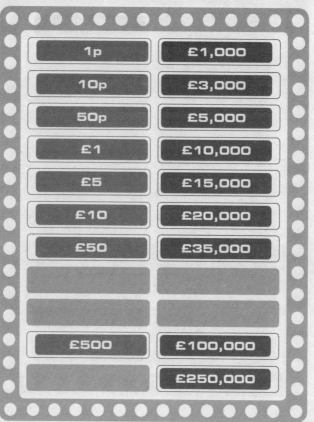

1p	£1,000
10p	£3,000
50p	£5,000
£1	£10,000
£5	£15,000
£10	£20,000
£50	£35,000
£500	£100,000
	£250,000

BANKER'S OFFER
£800

✗ NO DEAL

292

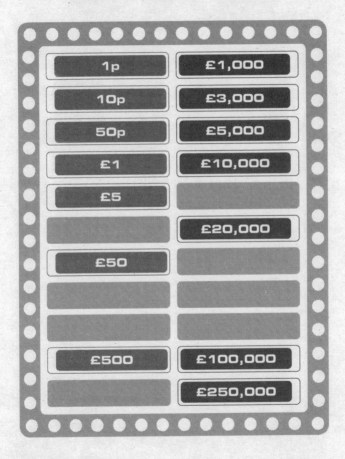

1p	£1,000
10p	£3,000
50p	£5,000
£1	£10,000
£5	
	£20,000
£50	
£500	£100,000
	£250,000

BANKER'S OFFER
£2,700

X NO DEAL

293

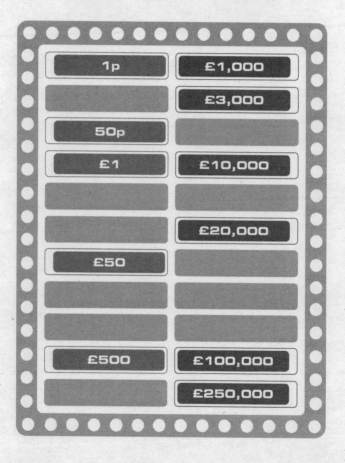

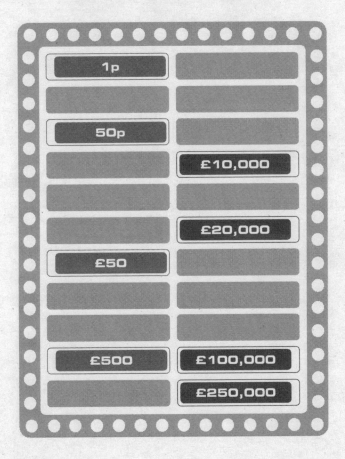

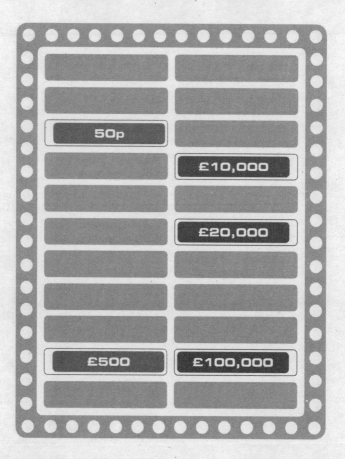

50p

£10,000

£20,000

£500   £100,000

BANKER'S OFFER
£11,000
Tick a box and turn to
page 393 for the answer.

✓ DEAL

✓ NO DEAL

£250	£500	£750	£1k	£75k
17	2	19	14	12

1p	
10p	£3,000
50p	£5,000
£1	£10,000
£5	£15,000
£10	£20,000
£50	£35,000
£100	£50,000
	£100,000
	£250,000

BANKER'S OFFER
£2,100

X NO DEAL

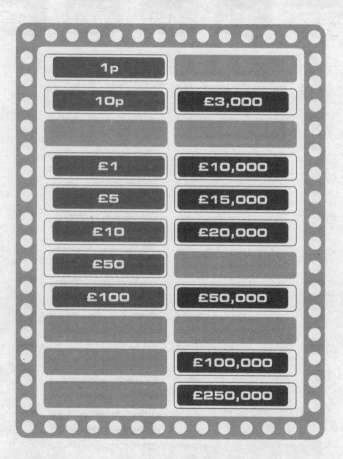

1p	
10p	£3,000
£1	£10,000
£5	£15,000
£10	£20,000
£50	
£100	£50,000
	£100,000
	£250,000

BANKER'S OFFER
£7,500

NO DEAL

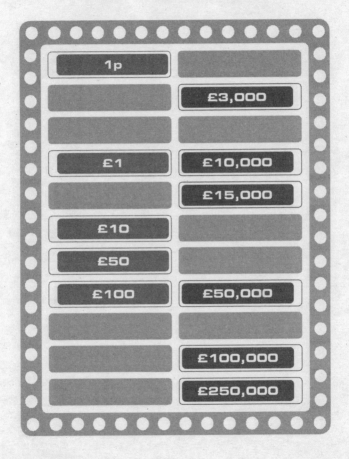

BANKER'S OFFER
£13,300

X **NO DEAL**

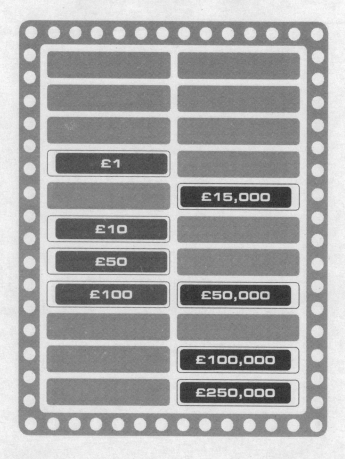

£1	
	£15,000
£10	
£50	
£100	£50,000
	£100,000
	£250,000

BANKER'S OFFER
£24,900

X NO DEAL

300

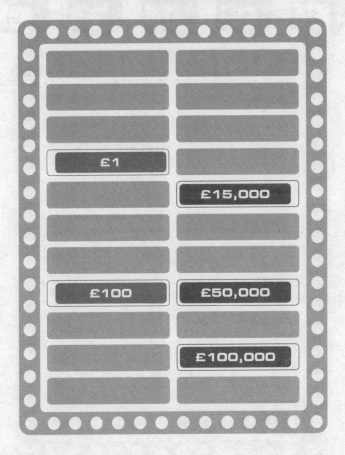

£1

£15,000

£100

£50,000

£100,000

BANKER'S OFFER

£18,000

Tick a box and turn to
page 394 for the answer.

✓ DEAL

✓ NO DEAL

GAME 14
CONTESTANT'S BOX

6

1p	£10	£1k	£3k	£250k
2	16	10	7	9

10p	
50p	£5,000
£1	£10,000
£5	£15,000
	£20,000
£50	£35,000
£100	£50,000
£250	£75,000
£500	£100,000
£750	

BANKER'S OFFER
£1,200

X NO DEAL

302

£250   £500   £100k
12   1   13

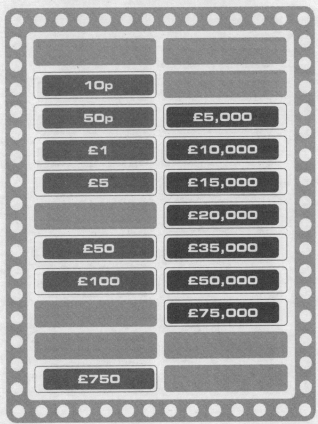

10p	
50p	£5,000
£1	£10,000
£5	£15,000
	£20,000
£50	£35,000
£100	£50,000
	£75,000
£750	

BANKER'S OFFER
£4,000

X NO DEAL

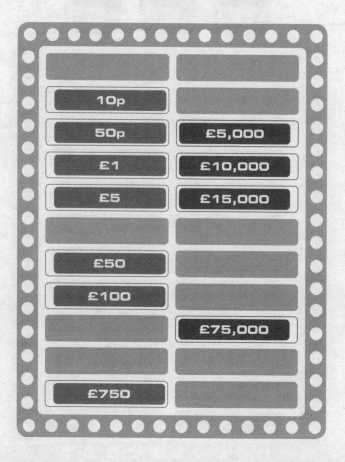

10p	
50p	£5,000
£1	£10,000
£5	£15,000
£50	
£100	
	£75,000
£750	

BANKER'S OFFER
£2,000

NO DEAL

10p — 14
£5 — 4
£100 — 5

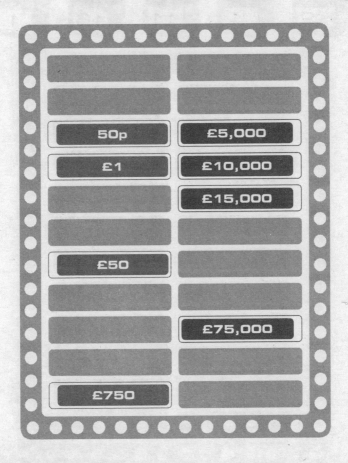

50p	£5,000
£1	£10,000
	£15,000
£50	
	£75,000
£750	

BANKER'S OFFER
£6,000
Tick a box and turn to page 394 for the answer.

✓ DEAL

✓ NO DEAL

GAME 15

CONTESTANT'S BOX 6

50p	£1	£500	£75k	£250k
12	4	11	16	1

1p	£1,000
10p	£3,000
	£5,000
	£10,000
£5	£15,000
£10	£20,000
£50	£35,000
£100	£50,000
£250	
	£100,000
£750	

BANKER'S OFFER
£1,300

✗ **NO DEAL**

306

£750 — 3

£1k — 22

£35k — 20

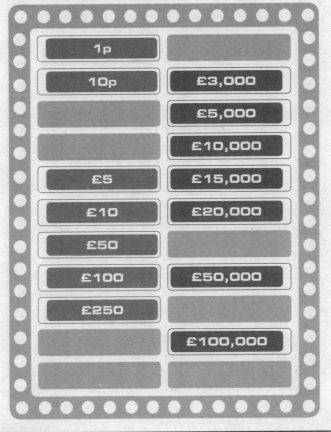

1p	
10p	£3,000
	£5,000
	£10,000
£5	£15,000
£10	£20,000
£50	
£100	£50,000
£250	
	£100,000

BANKER'S OFFER
£4,600

X NO DEAL

307

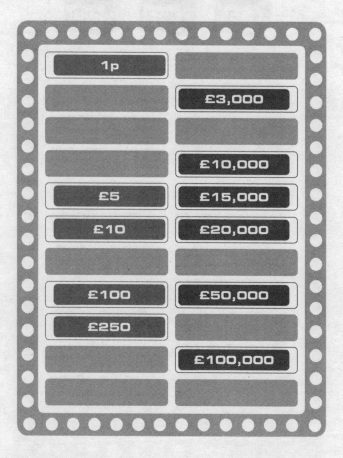

1p	
	£3,000
	£10,000
£5	£15,000
£10	£20,000
£100	£50,000
£250	
	£100,000

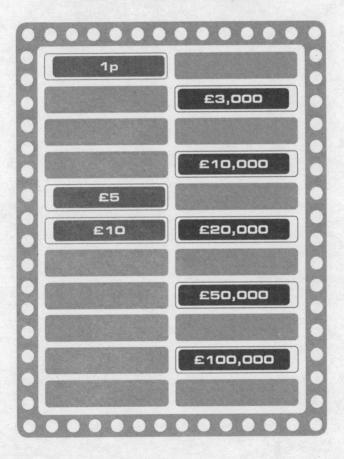

1p

£3,000

£10,000

£5

£10

£20,000

£50,000

£100,000

BANKER'S OFFER
£19,000
Tick a box and turn to
page 394 for the answer.

✓ DEAL

✓ NO DEAL

CHAPTER 07
BEAT THE BANKER:
EXPERT

So you're here. You're going to play the expert version of the most challenging game in the book. It's Beat The Banker, and it's now or never. I can't help you any more. You are on your own.

Before you start, before that telephone starts ringing again for the last time, take a moment to reflect on all that you have learned. Do you have a better understanding of The Banker's cunning than when you started? Do you get flustered, especially when you're against the clock? Or do you think you have got the better of him, cracked his code, figured him out? Many have tried, many brave contestants have faced him down. But it's like looking into the eyes of a cobra. Beware! Don't be overconfident! If you keep your nerve, if you have in your mind all that you went through to get to this point, you can do it, you can beat The Banker.

Keep your score as before, and see his reaction at the end. If you do pull it off, I'll tell you this. He won't be pleased. And if you lose, he'll laugh. Don't give him that pleasure. Pick up the phone. It's time. Deal Or No Deal.

GAME 01
CONTESTANT'S BOX

5

1p	£5	£50k	£75k	£100k
1	3	6	7	19

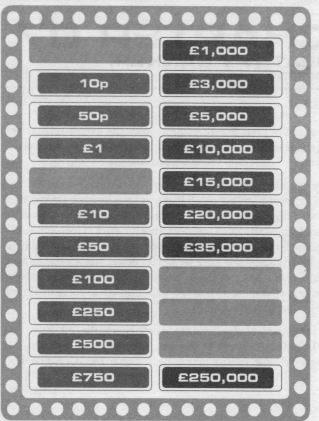

	£1,000
10p	£3,000
50p	£5,000
£1	£10,000
	£15,000
£10	£20,000
£50	£35,000
£100	
£250	
£500	
£750	£250,000

BANKER'S OFFER
£800

X NO DEAL

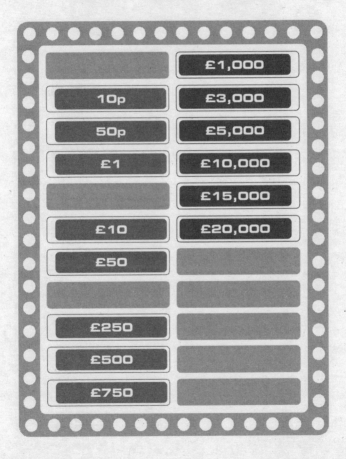

BANKER'S OFFER £200

X NO DEAL

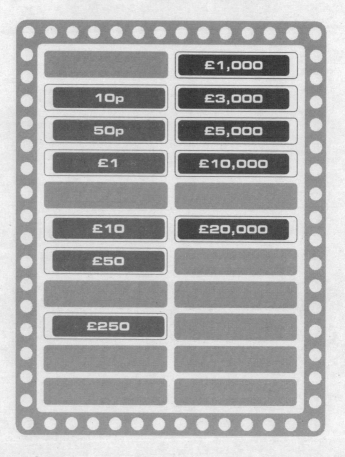

£250 **16**   £3k **15**   £10k **8**

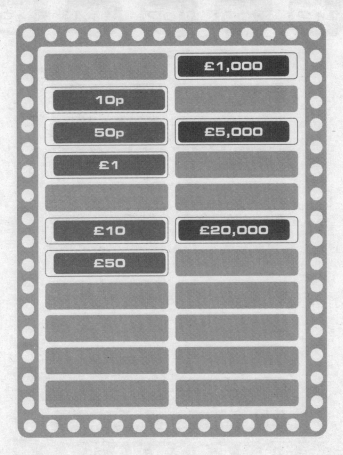

	£1,000
10p	
50p	£5,000
£1	
£10	£20,000
£50	

BANKER'S OFFER

£1,000

Tick a box and turn to page 395 for the answer.

✓ DEAL

✓ NO DEAL

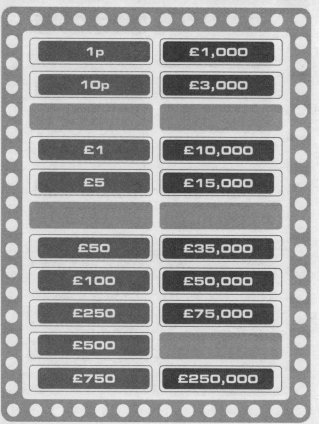

50p	£10	£5k	£20k	£100k
12	20	22	14	19

1p	£1,000
10p	£3,000
£1	£10,000
£5	£15,000
£50	£35,000
£100	£50,000
£250	£75,000
£500	
£750	£250,000

BANKER'S OFFER
£2,200

X NO DEAL

318

1p	£1,000
10p	£3,000
£1	
	£15,000
£50	£35,000
£100	£50,000
£250	
£500	
£750	£250,000

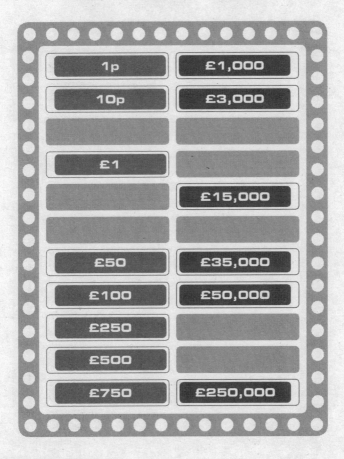

BANKER'S OFFER
£4,700

X **NO DEAL**

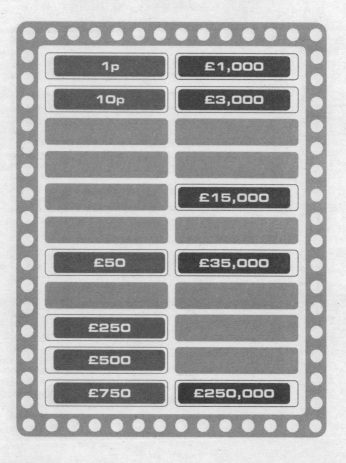

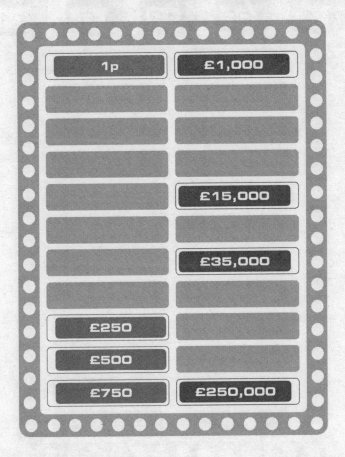

1p	£1,000
	£15,000
	£35,000
£250	
£500	
£750	£250,000

BANKER'S OFFER
£13,000
Tick a box and turn to page 395 for the answer.

✓ DEAL

✓ NO DEAL

£1	£10k	£15k	£20k	£75k
4	22	12	6	21

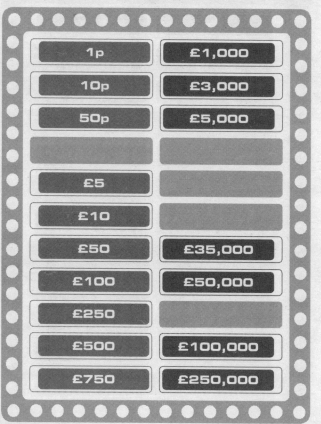

1p	£1,000
10p	£3,000
50p	£5,000
£5	
£10	
£50	£35,000
£100	£50,000
£250	
£500	£100,000
£750	£250,000

BANKER'S OFFER
£7,500

✗ NO DEAL

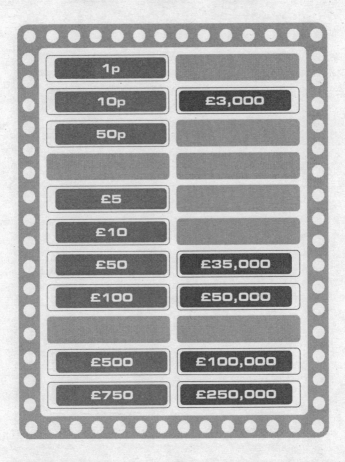

1p	
10p	£3,000
50p	
£5	
£10	
£50	£35,000
£100	£50,000
£500	£100,000
£750	£250,000

BANKER'S OFFER
£1,500

X NO DEAL

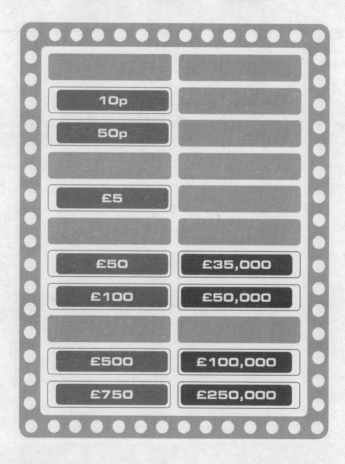

BANKER'S OFFER
£22,700
Tick a box and turn to
page 395 for the answer.

✓ DEAL

✓ NO DEAL

GAME 04
CONTESTANT'S BOX

16

£10	£50	£1k	£10k	£100k
11	2	1	7	5

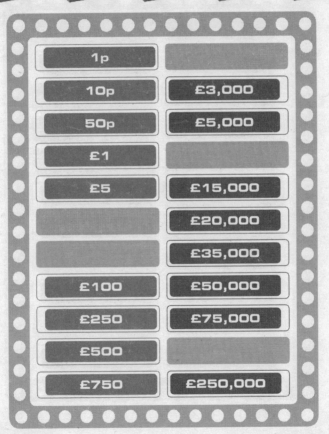

1p	
10p	£3,000
50p	£5,000
£1	
£5	£15,000
	£20,000
	£35,000
£100	£50,000
£250	£75,000
£500	
£750	£250,000

BANKER'S OFFER
£6,000

X NO DEAL

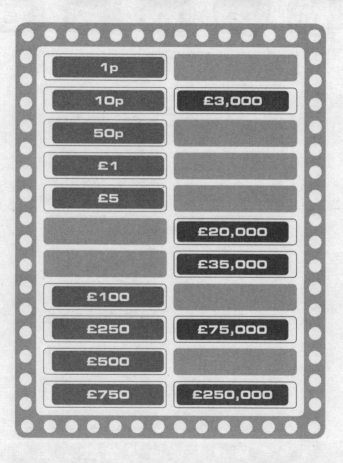

1p	
10p	£3,000
50p	
£1	
£5	
	£20,000
	£35,000
£100	
£250	£75,000
£500	
£750	£250,000

BANKER'S OFFER £3,000

X NO DEAL

326

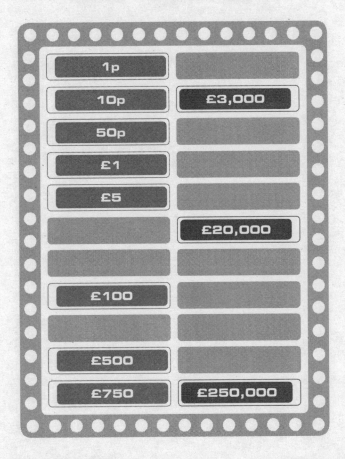

BANKER'S OFFER
£12,000

X NO DEAL

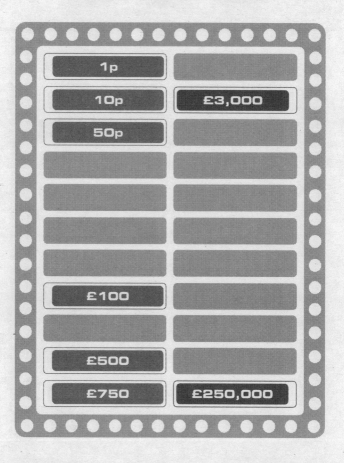

BANKER'S OFFER
£17,800
Tick a box and turn to
page 396 for the answer.

✓ DEAL

✓ NO DEAL

GAME 05

CONTESTANT'S BOX

7

50p	£10	£5k	£20k	£100k
12	20	22	14	19

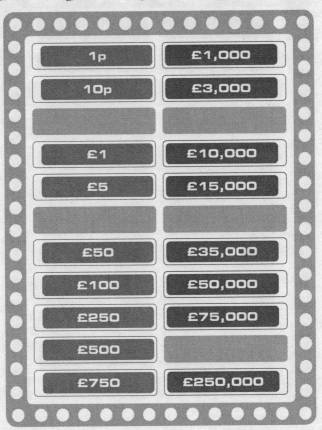

1p	£1,000
10p	£3,000
£1	£10,000
£5	£15,000
£50	£35,000
£100	£50,000
£250	£75,000
£500	
£750	£250,000

BANKER'S OFFER
£2,200

X **NO DEAL**

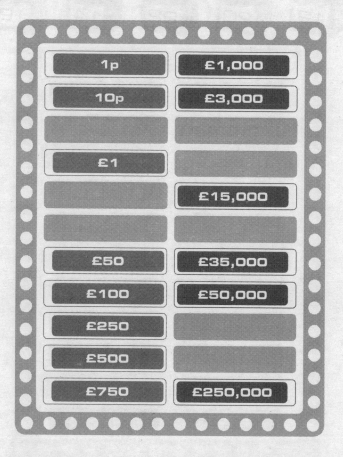

1p	£1,000
10p	£3,000
£1	
	£15,000
£50	£35,000
£100	£50,000
£250	
£500	
£750	£250,000

BANKER'S OFFER
£4,700

X **NO DEAL**

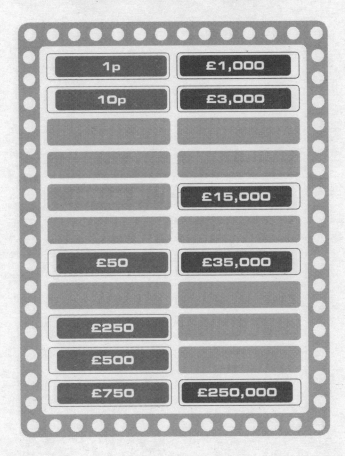

1p	£1,000
10p	£3,000
	£15,000
£50	£35,000
£250	
£500	
£750	£250,000

BANKER'S OFFER
£3,000

X NO DEAL

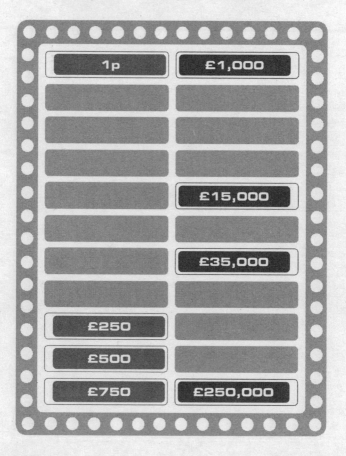

1p	£1,000
	£15,000
	£35,000
£250	
£500	
£750	£250,000

BANKER'S OFFER
£13,000

X NO DEAL

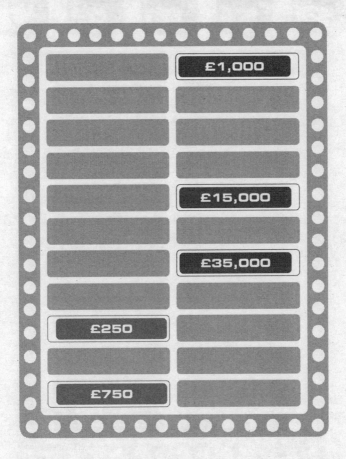

£1,000

£15,000

£35,000

£250

£750

BANKER'S OFFER

£4,000

Tick a box and turn to
page 396 for the answer.

✓ DEAL

✓ NO DEAL

1p	10p	£3k	£5k	£20k
2	1	14	19	7

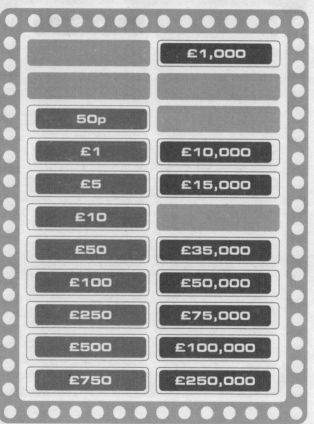

	£1,000
50p	
£1	£10,000
£5	£15,000
£10	
£50	£35,000
£100	£50,000
£250	£75,000
£500	£100,000
£750	£250,000

BANKER'S OFFER
£7,000

X **NO DEAL**

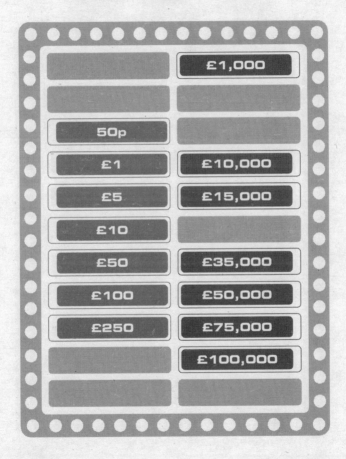

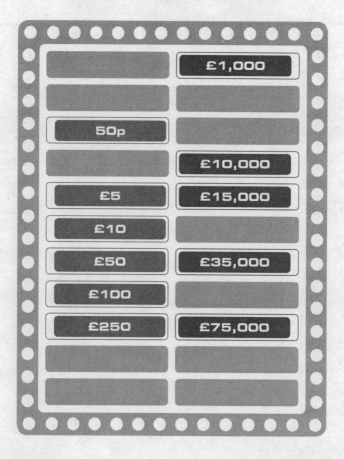

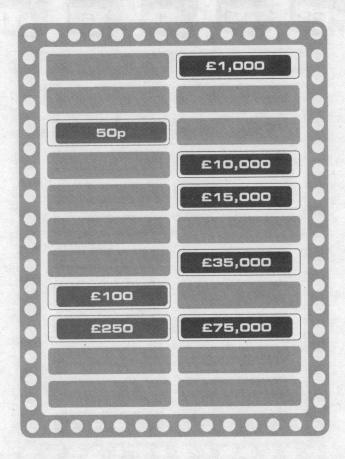

BANKER'S OFFER
£11,700

Tick a box and turn to
page 396 for the answer.

✓ DEAL

✓ NO DEAL

GAME 07
CONTESTANT'S BOX

3

£1	£5	£750	£1k	£100k
22	13	1	6	11

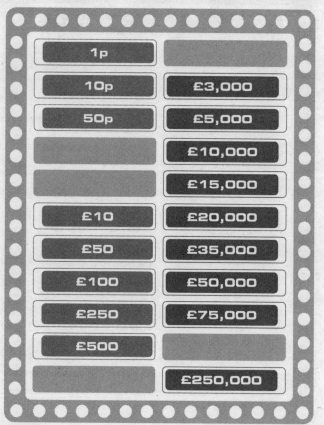

1p	
10p	£3,000
50p	£5,000
	£10,000
	£15,000
£10	£20,000
£50	£35,000
£100	£50,000
£250	£75,000
£500	
	£250,000

BANKER'S OFFER
£6,200

X **NO DEAL**

338

1p	
10p	£3,000
50p	£5,000
	£10,000
	£15,000
	£20,000
£50	£35,000
£100	
£250	
£500	
	£250,000

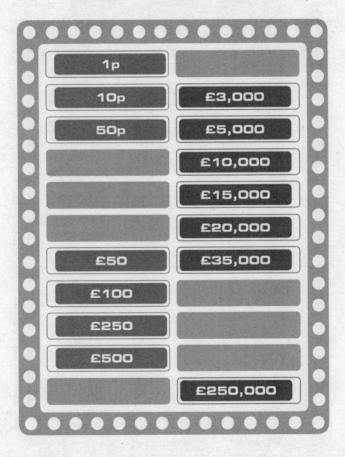

 BANKER'S OFFER
£2,000

 **X NO DEAL**

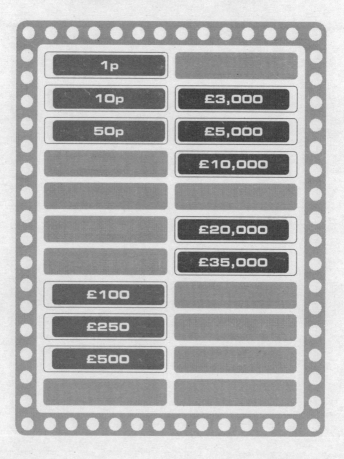

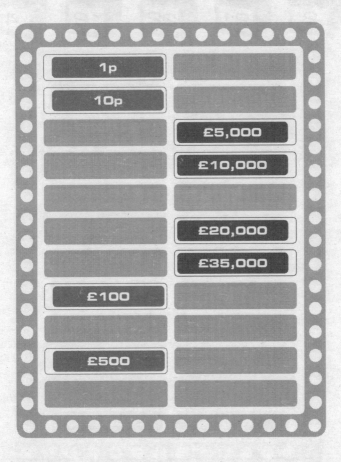

1p	
10p	
	£5,000
	£10,000
	£20,000
	£35,000
£100	
£500	

BANKER'S OFFER

£4,400

Tick a box and turn to
page 397 for the answer.

✓ DEAL

✓ NO DEAL

GAME 08
CONTESTANT'S BOX

16

10p **2**	£500 **21**	£15k **22**	£75k **12**	£100k **4**

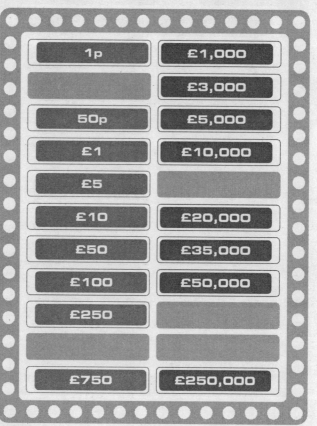

1p	£1,000
	£3,000
50p	£5,000
£1	£10,000
£5	
£10	£20,000
£50	£35,000
£100	£50,000
£250	
£750	£250,000

BANKER'S OFFER
£1,100

X NO DEAL

342

£10	£50	£250k
17	20	7

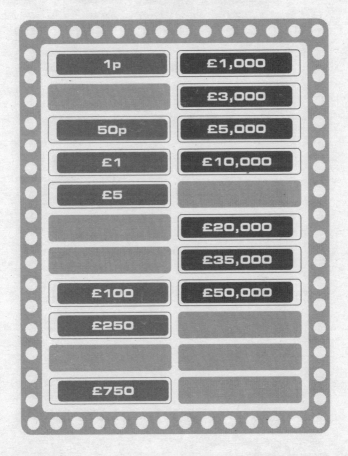

1p	£1,000
	£3,000
50p	£5,000
£1	£10,000
£5	
	£20,000
	£35,000
£100	£50,000
£250	
£750	

BANKER'S OFFER
£300

X **NO DEAL**

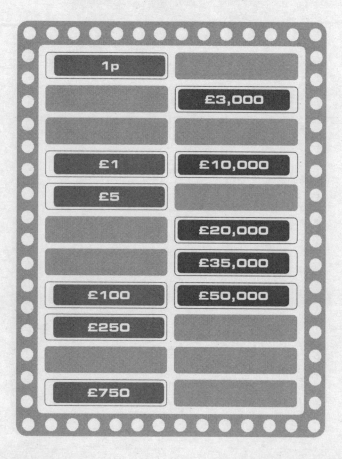

1p	
	£3,000
£1	£10,000
£5	
	£20,000
	£35,000
£100	£50,000
£250	
£750	

BANKER'S OFFER
£5,300

344

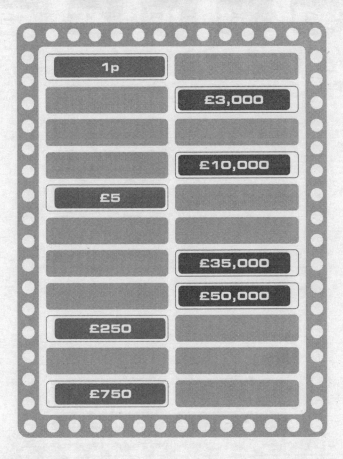

1p	
	£3,000
	£10,000
£5	
	£35,000
	£50,000
£250	
£750	

BANKER'S OFFER

£8,100

Tick a box and turn to
page 397 for the answer.

✓ DEAL

✓ NO DEAL

GAME 09

CONTESTANT'S BOX — 18

10p — 9	£50 — 5	£100 — 15	£35k — 1	£75k — 19

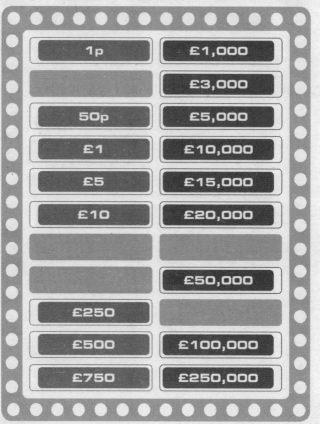

1p	£1,000
	£3,000
50p	£5,000
£1	£10,000
£5	£15,000
£10	£20,000
	£50,000
£250	
£500	£100,000
£750	£250,000

BANKER'S OFFER
£3,200

X NO DEAL

346

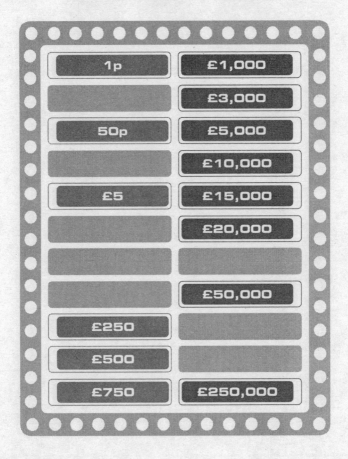

1p	£1,000
	£3,000
50p	£5,000
	£10,000
£5	£15,000
	£20,000
	£50,000
£250	
£500	
£750	£250,000

BANKER'S OFFER
£3,200

X NO DEAL

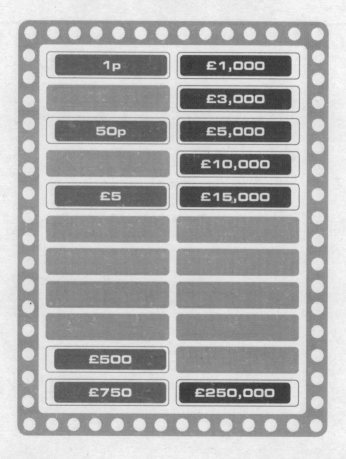

BANKER'S OFFER
£1,600

NO DEAL

£5 — 3
£1k — 10
£5k — 12

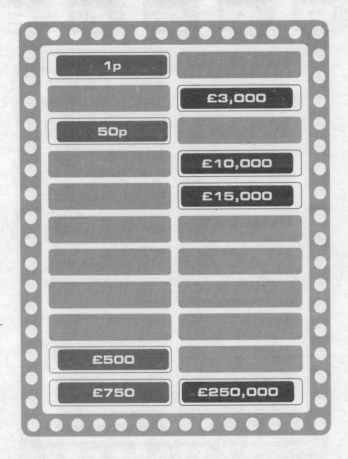

1p

£3,000

50p

£10,000

£15,000

£500

£750

£250,000

BANKER'S OFFER
£9,600
Tick a box and turn to page 397 for the answer.

✓ DEAL

✓ NO DEAL

GAME 10

CONTESTANT'S BOX

21

£50	£750	£1k	£3k	£35k
7	1	17	4	2

1p	
10p	
50p	£5,000
£1	£10,000
£5	£15,000
£10	£20,000
£100	£50,000
£250	£75,000
£500	£100,000
	£250,000

BANKER'S OFFER
£4,000

X NO DEAL

2 MINUTE TIME CHALLENGE
Try and answer this question in 2 minutes.

50p — 13
£5k — 11
£20k — 20

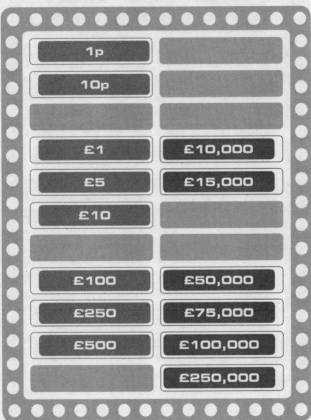

1p	
10p	
£1	£10,000
£5	£15,000
£10	
£100	£50,000
£250	£75,000
£500	£100,000
	£250,000

BANKER'S OFFER
£10,000

X NO DEAL

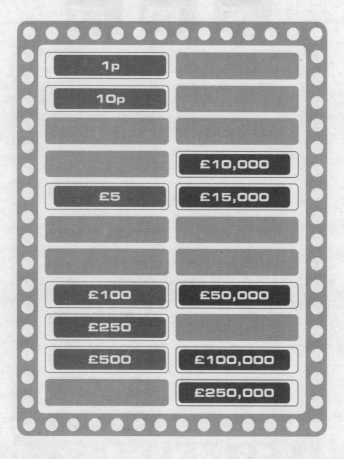

1p	
10p	
	£10,000
£5	£15,000
£100	£50,000
£250	
£500	£100,000
	£250,000

BANKER'S OFFER
£7,000

X **NO DEAL**

£100
16

£15k
18

£250k
15

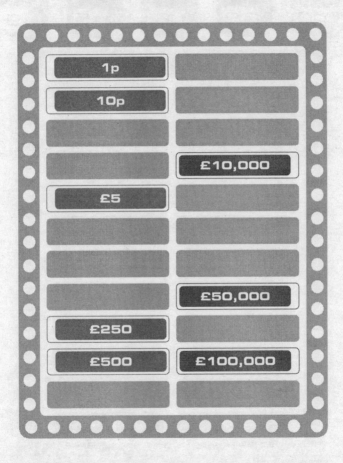

1p

10p

£10,000

£5

£50,000

£250

£500

£100,000

BANKER'S OFFER

£12,000

Tick a box and turn to
page 398 for the answer.

✓ DEAL

✓ NO DEAL

GAME 11
CONTESTANT'S BOX 2

1p	£1	£1k	£10k	£100k
20	13	6	15	9

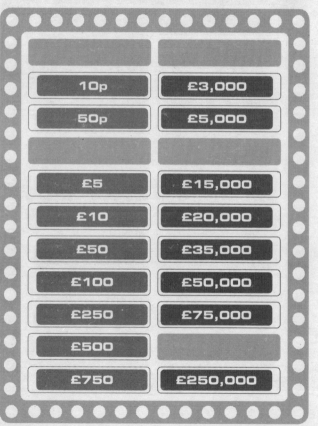

10p	£3,000
50p	£5,000
£5	£15,000
£10	£20,000
£50	£35,000
£100	£50,000
£250	£75,000
£500	
£750	£250,000

BANKER'S OFFER
£7,000

X NO DEAL

2 MINUTE TIME CHALLENGE
Try and answer this question in 2 minutes.

£750 — 14
£20k — 12
£50k — 10

10p	£3,000
50p	£5,000
£5	£15,000
£10	
£50	£35,000
£100	
£250	£75,000
£500	
	£250,000

BANKER'S OFFER
£3,500

X NO DEAL

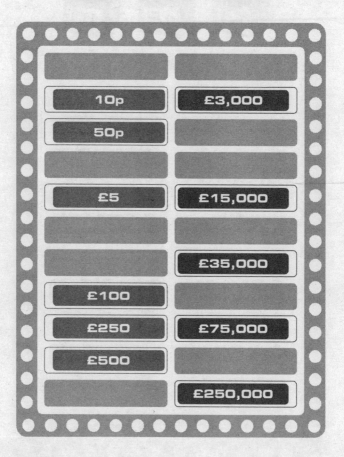

10p	£3,000
50p	
£5	£15,000
	£35,000
£100	
£250	£75,000
£500	
	£250,000

BANKER'S OFFER
£13,500

X NO DEAL

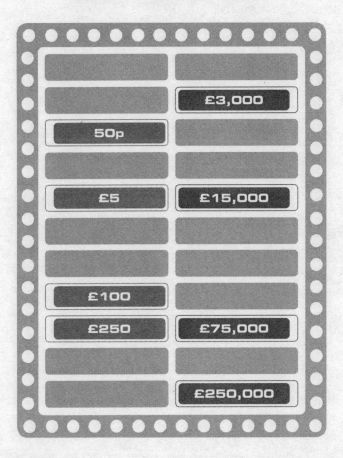

 BANKER'S OFFER
£27,000

X NO DEAL

£5 £100 £15k
18   17   1

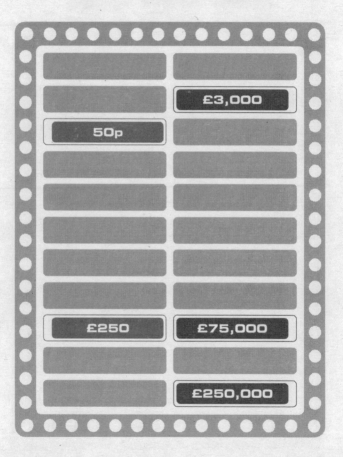

£3,000

50p

£250   £75,000

£250,000

BANKER'S OFFER
£63,000
Tick a box and turn to
page 398 for the answer.

✓ DEAL

✓ NO DEAL

GAME 12
CONTESTANT'S BOX

9

1p	50p	£100	£50k	£75k
5	10	18	17	7

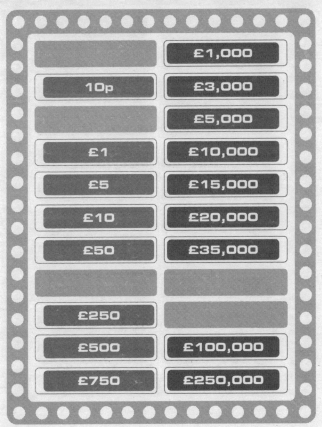

	£1,000
10p	£3,000
	£5,000
£1	£10,000
£5	£15,000
£10	£20,000
£50	£35,000
£250	
£500	£100,000
£750	£250,000

BANKER'S OFFER
£1,300

✗ NO DEAL

359

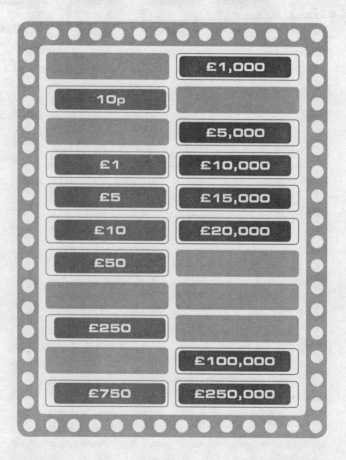

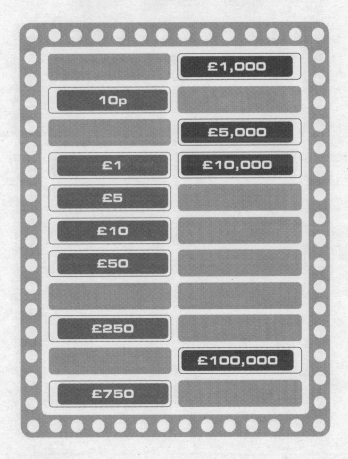

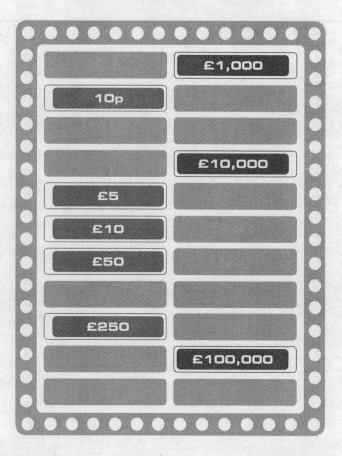

BANKER'S OFFER
£8,100

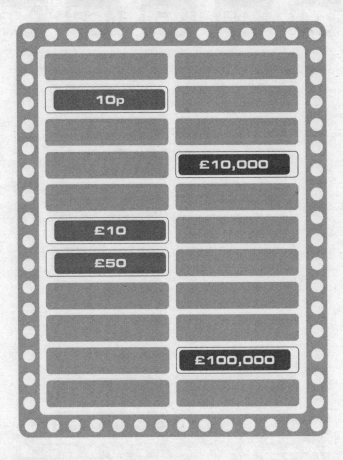

GAME 13

CONTESTANT'S BOX

3

1p	£50	£500	£750	£75k
11	19	5	22	18

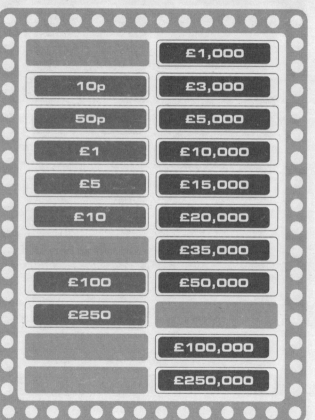

	£1,000
10p	£3,000
50p	£5,000
£1	£10,000
£5	£15,000
£10	£20,000
	£35,000
£100	£50,000
£250	
	£100,000
	£250,000

BANKER'S OFFER £3,100

X **NO DEAL**

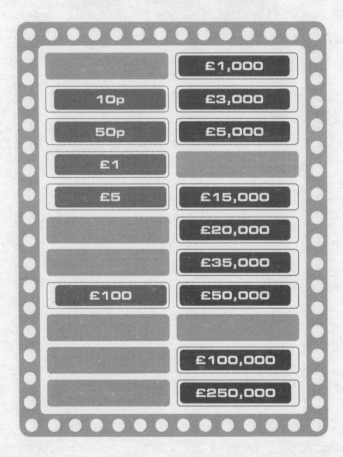

	£1,000
10p	£3,000
50p	£5,000
£1	
£5	£15,000
	£20,000
	£35,000
£100	£50,000
	£100,000
	£250,000

BANKER'S OFFER
£12,600

X NO DEAL

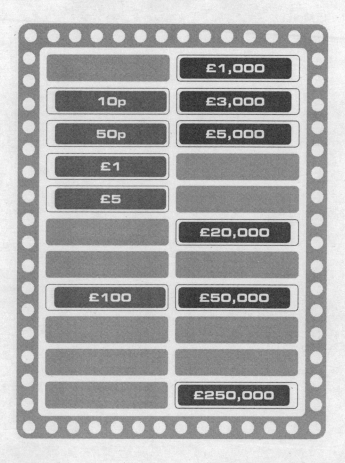

	£1,000
10p	£3,000
£1	
	£20,000
£100	£50,000
	£250,000

BANKER'S OFFER
£1,700

X NO DEAL

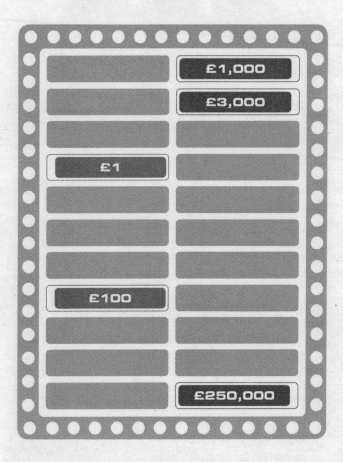

£1,000

£3,000

£1

£100

£250,000

BANKER'S OFFER
£47,000
Tick a box and turn to
page 399 for the answer.

368

GAME 14
CONTESTANT'S BOX

10

£1	£100	£500	£1k	£250k
21	11	9	7	12

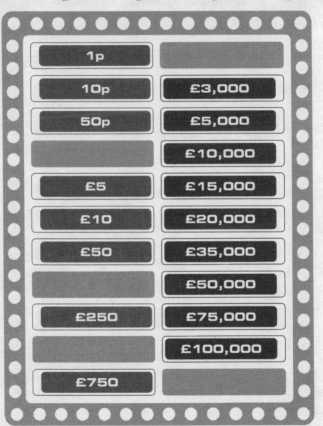

1p	
10p	£3,000
50p	£5,000
	£10,000
£5	£15,000
£10	£20,000
£50	£35,000
	£50,000
£250	£75,000
	£100,000
£750	

BANKER'S OFFER
£500

X NO DEAL

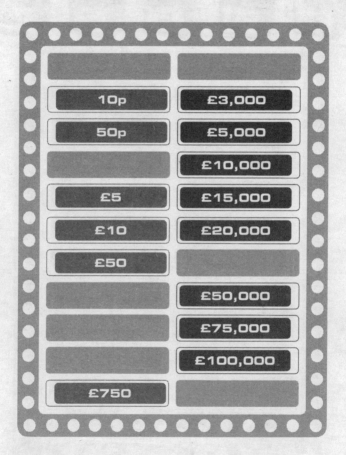

10p	£3,000
50p	£5,000
	£10,000
£5	£15,000
£10	£20,000
£50	
	£50,000
	£75,000
	£100,000
£750	

BANKER'S OFFER
£4,000

X **NO DEAL**

370

50p	£5,000
	£10,000
£5	£15,000
£10	£20,000
£50	
	£50,000
	£100,000
£750	

BANKER'S OFFER
£9,000

X **NO DEAL**

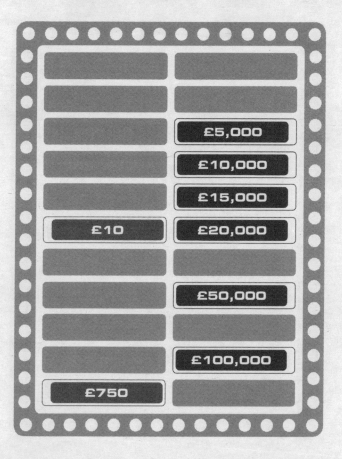

BANKER'S OFFER
£16,500

Tick a box and turn to
page 399 for the answer.

DEAL

NO DEAL

GAME 15
CONTESTANT'S BOX

1

1p **7**	£50 **13**
£250 **5**	£5k **10**
£15k **3**	

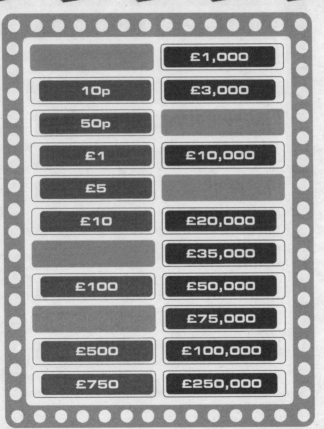

	£1,000
10p	£3,000
50p	
£1	£10,000
£5	
£10	£20,000
	£35,000
£100	£50,000
	£75,000
£500	£100,000
£750	£250,000

BANKER'S OFFER £4,100

X NO DEAL

373

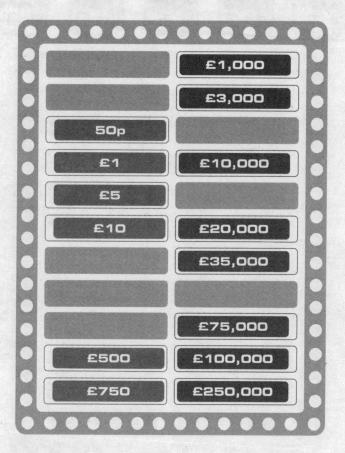

	£1,000
	£3,000
50p	
£1	£10,000
£5	
£10	£20,000
	£35,000
	£75,000
£500	£100,000
£750	£250,000

BANKER'S OFFER
£8,200

X NO DEAL

374

	£1,000
	£3,000
£1	£10,000
£5	
£10	
	£35,000
	£75,000
£500	£100,000
	£250,000

 BANKER'S OFFER £2,400   X **NO DEAL**

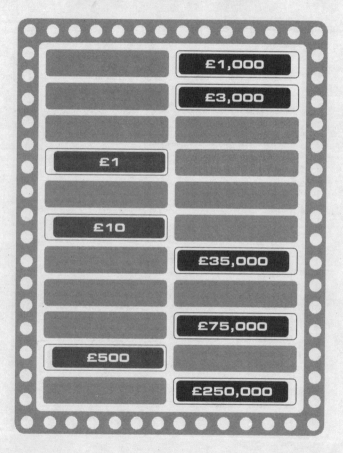

BANKER'S OFFER
£20,000
Tick a box and turn to
page 399 for the answer.

✓ DEAL

✓ NO DEAL

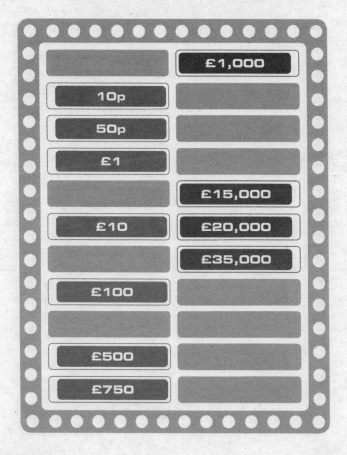

	£1,000
10p	
50p	
£1	
	£15,000
£10	£20,000
	£35,000
£100	
£500	
£750	

BANKER'S OFFER
£1,300

X NO DEAL

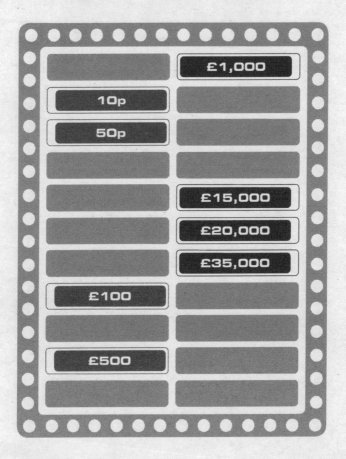

	£1,000
10p	
50p	
	£15,000
	£20,000
	£35,000
£100	
£500	

BANKER'S OFFER

£4,000

Tick a box and turn to
page 399 for the answer.

✓ DEAL

✓ NO DEAL

380

ANSWERS
OPENING OFFERS

The correct answers are in bold. Award yourself one mark for every right answer. Once you have added them up read how The Banker thinks you got on.

GAME 01	**A. £4,300**	B. £52,800	C. £11,000	
GAME 02	A. £95,000	B. £50	**C. £3,100**	
GAME 03	**A. £1,100**	B. £8,000	C. £70,000	
GAME 04	A. £8,700	**B. £6,300**	C. £12,000	
GAME 05	**A. £800**	B. £200	C. £100	
GAME 06	A. £5,300	**B. £2,100**	C. £4,000	
GAME 07	A. £10,200	**B. £1,200**	C. £6,600	
GAME 08	**A. £700**	B. £200	C. £1,600	
GAME 09	A. £12,000	B. £15,000	**C. £1,300**	
GAME 10	A. £14,400	B. £2,000	**C. £7,000**	
GAME 11	A. £8,600	B. £4,700	**C. £1,300**	
GAME 12	A. £2,000	**B. £3,300**	C. £5,600	
GAME 13	**A. £3,100**	B. £8,000	C. £12,900	
GAME 14	A. £6,500	B. £2,500	**C. £500**	
GAME 15	**A. £4,100**	B. £9,000	C. £1,200	
GAME 16	**A. £3,000**	B. £6,900	C. £10,500	
			TOTAL	

THE BANKER SAYS..

Low scores (1-4)
I like you. I like you a lot. You are absolutely hopeless.
Keep playing, but maybe think about taking your socks
and shoes off for the next round, you obviously need
help counting beyond ten.

Medium scores (5-10)
This was the first round. It was supposed to be easy.
The chimpanzee I tried it out on thought so, anyway.

High scores (10-16)
The first, very simple round. OK, you did quite well,
but frankly I expected everyone to do this well.
So maybe you're not as clever as you think.

ANSWERS
GUESS THE NEXT OFFER:
BEGINNER

The correct answers are in bold. Award yourself one mark for every right answer. Once you have added them up read how The Banker thinks you got on.

GAME 01	A. £25,000	B. £32,000	**C. £7,300**	
GAME 02	A. £10,000	B. £20,000	**C. £30,000**	
GAME 03	**A. £4,700**	B. £500	C. £1,000	
GAME 04	A. £9,500	**B. £4,500**	C. £10,000	
GAME 05	**A. £42,000**	B. £28,000	C. £50,000	
GAME 06	A. £20,000	B. £4,321	**C. £12,000**	
GAME 07	**A. £6,000**	B. £600	C. £60,000	
GAME 08	A. £12,000	B. £3,000	**C. £6,000**	
GAME 09	**A. £1,300**	B. £14,500	C. £18,000	
GAME 10	A. £5,000	B. £21,000	**C. £1,500**	
			TOTAL	

THE BANKER SAYS..

Low scores (1-3)

That round was a little bit trickier and with you, it shows! Keep it up, and think of all the things you could do with 1p!

Medium scores (4-6)

Average to me means boring. You're not a complete idiot – I like them! – but you're still going home on the bus.

High scores (7-10)

It's still early. You show some promise, but so many promises are broken!

ANSWERS
GUESS THE NEXT OFFER:
EXPERT

The correct answers are in bold. Award yourself one mark for every right answer. Once you have added them up read how The Banker thinks you got on.

GAME 01	A. £8,900	**B. £9,900**	C. £6,400
GAME 02	**A. £12,000**	B. £7,100	C. £17,000
GAME 03	**A. £21,000**	B. £18,000	C. £24,000
GAME 04	A. £220	**B. £400**	C. £380
GAME 05	A. £12,000	B. £24,000	**C. £18,000**
GAME 06	**A. £7,200**	B. £9,000	C. £10,000
GAME 07	A. £8,000	B. £2,000	**C. £4,500**
GAME 08	**A. £7,100**	B. £11,000	C. £14,500
GAME 09	A. £13,500	**B. £21,000**	C. £19,000
GAME 10	A. £17,800	**B. £14,500**	C. £19,400
			TOTAL

THE BANKER SAYS..

Low scores (1-3)

I like my money. With you playing, I have no chance of losing it. Why not get your friends to play too!

Medium scores (4-6)

Your very average performance suggests that my cash is not at risk. The spiders on my wallet slumber on, untroubled.

High scores (7-10)

You may think you are quite smart. Well, let me tell you. Cheating is neither big, nor clever. Anyway, there's still a long way to go.

ANSWERS
TOTALISER:
BEGINNER

GAME				TOTAL
01	**01** £2,900	**02** £4,000	**03** £11,500	**A.**
	04 £22,000	**05** £33,000		**£73,400**
02	**01** £3,900	**02** £7,100	**03** £6,500	**A.**
	04 £1,300	**05** £35,000		**£53,800**
03	**01** £6,900	**02** £1,600	**03** £4,800	**C.**
	04 £14,800	**05** £28,000	**06** £4,800	**£60,900**
04	**01** £700	**02** £1,800	**03** £7,400	**C.**
	04 £9,500	**05** £18,500		**£37,900**
05	**01** £2,300	**02** £6,100	**03** £14,500	**B.**
	04 £33,000	**05** £52,000	**06** £120,000	**£227,900**
06	**01** £1,000	**02** £4,000	**03** £7,200	**A.**
	04 £8,600	**05** £10,100		**£30,900**
07	**01** £900	**02** £1,500	**03** £6,000	**B.**
	04 £8,500	**05** £5,000	**06** £9,900	**£31,800**
08	**01** £1,400	**02** £2,100	**03** £900	**C.**
	04 £3,000	**05** £3,500		**£10,900**
09	**01** £2,100	**02** £1,500	**03** £6,900	**A.**
	04 £8,400	**05** £25,000		**£43,900**
10	**01** £500	**02** £1,500	**03** £2,500	**C.**
	04 £2,000	**05** £4,000		**£10,500**

THE BANKER SAYS..

Low scores (1-3)

You know, I think I'll put in another swimming pool.
And there's nothing you can do to stop me, is there?

Medium scores (4-6)

Sorry! I must have nodded off for a bit.
Did you have an exciting round?

High scores (7-10)

I see you growing more confident. Pride comes
before a fall, my friend, and you're going down.

ANSWERS
TOTALISER:
EXPERT

GAME				TOTAL
01	01 £1,000 04 £1,000	02 £500 05 £3,800	03 £1,400 06 £11,000	B. £7,700
02	01 £1,400 04 £18,500	02 £4,500	03 £7,900	B. £32,300
03	01 £9,000 04 £4,600	02 £900	03 £6,600	A. £21,100
04	01 £1,100 04 £4,000	02 £5,200 05 £7,500	03 £18,000	A. £35,800
05	01 £3,200 04 £2,700	02 £1,500	03 £1,900	C. £9,300
06	01 £800 04 £3,500	02 £3,200 05 £7,000	03 £2,200	B. £16,700
07	01 £1,300 04 £4,900	02 £2,900 05 £6,500	03 £700	A. £16,300
08	01 £300 04 £2,300	02 £1,200 05 £7,000	03 £4,700	B. £15,500

THE BANKER SAYS..

Low scores (1-3)

It's getting harder, isn't it? Not that it makes any difference to you. I wonder if you know what day it is?

Medium scores (4-5)

The way you play I'd guess you were an accountant, but they're supposed to be quite good at numbers, aren't they?

High scores (6-8)

You are beginning to irritate me. You are confident and a bit flashy, but I suspect you're a flash in the pan!

ANSWERS
BEAT THE BANKER:
BEGINNER

GAME 01

The correct answer was **DEAL.**
This was the highest offer The Banker made.

ROUND 04	BOX 11	BOX 4	BOX 18
AMOUNT	£100	£35,000	£250,000

BANKER'S OFFER : £2,500

ROUND 05	BOX 14	BOX 3	BOX 12
AMOUNT	1p	£10,000	£20,000

BANKER'S OFFER : £3,600

ROUND 06	BOX 2	BOX 15	BOX 9
AMOUNT	£50	£5,000	£15,000

BANKER'S OFFER : £1,200

GAME 02

The correct answer was **NO DEAL.**
More money was to be won on ROUND 05.

ROUND 05	BOX 21	BOX 14	BOX 20
AMOUNT	£50	£1,000	£75,000

BANKER'S OFFER : £12,400

ROUND 06	BOX 16	BOX 22	BOX 18
AMOUNT	£15,000	£35,000	£50,000

BANKER'S OFFER : £40

GAME 03

The correct answer was **DEAL.**
This was the highest offer The Banker made.

ROUND 06	BOX 12	BOX 2	BOX 14
AMOUNT	£10	£100	£100,000

BANKER'S OFFER : £2,000

GAME 04

The correct answer was **NO DEAL.**
More money was to be won on ROUND 05.

ROUND 05	BOX 19	BOX 21	BOX 12
AMOUNT	£100	£250	£15,000

BANKER'S OFFER : £18,000

ROUND 06	BOX 22	BOX 1	BOX 10
AMOUNT	£50	£75,000	£100,000

BANKER'S OFFER : £1,800

GAME 05

The correct answer was **NO DEAL.**
More money was to be won on ROUND 05.

ROUND 05	BOX 12	BOX 14	BOX 16
AMOUNT	£750	£1,000	£3,000

BANKER'S OFFER : £55,000

ROUND 06	BOX 19	BOX 21	BOX 20
AMOUNT	1p	50p	£250,000

BANKER'S OFFER : £7,000

GAME 06

The correct answer was **NO DEAL.**
More money was to be won on ROUND 06.

ROUND 05	BOX 17	BOX 22	BOX 16
AMOUNT	1p	£500	£100,000

BANKER'S OFFER : £23,000

ROUND 06	BOX 15	BOX 20	BOX 14
AMOUNT	50p	£5,000	£35,000

BANKER'S OFFER : £37,000

GAME 07

The correct answer was **DEAL.**
This was the highest offer The Banker made.

ROUND 06	BOX 18	BOX 20	BOX 22
AMOUNT	£10	£20,000	£250,000

BANKER'S OFFER : £1,200

GAME 08

The correct answer was **DEAL.**
This was the highest offer The Banker made.

ROUND 05	BOX 10	BOX 15	BOX 13
AMOUNT	£5	£15,000	£250,000

BANKER'S OFFER : £6,000

ROUND 06	BOX 21	BOX 22	BOX 4
AMOUNT	10p	£5,000	£50,000

BANKER'S OFFER : £4

GAME 09

The correct answer was **DEAL.**
This was the highest offer The Banker made.

ROUND 05	BOX 17	BOX 11	BOX 2
AMOUNT	£5,000	£15,000	£100,000

BANKER'S OFFER : £80

ROUND 06	BOX 7	BOX 6	BOX 12
AMOUNT	£5	£500	£750

BANKER'S OFFER : £20

GAME 10

The correct answer was **DEAL.**
This was the highest offer The Banker made.

ROUND 05	BOX 7	BOX 12	BOX 15
AMOUNT	£20,000	£50,000	£100,000

BANKER'S OFFER : £900

GAME 11

The correct answer was **NO DEAL.**
More money was to be won on ROUND 06.

ROUND 06	BOX 9	BOX 15	BOX 16
AMOUNT	50p	£5	£1,000

BANKER'S OFFER : £175,000

GAME 12

The correct answer was **NO DEAL.**
More money was to be won on ROUND 06.

ROUND 06	BOX 10	BOX 9	BOX 7
AMOUNT	50p	£500	£20,000

BANKER'S OFFER : £50,000

GAME 13

The correct answer was **NO DEAL.**
More money was to be won on ROUND 06.

ROUND 06	BOX 22	BOX 7	BOX 18
AMOUNT	£1	£15,000	£50,000

BANKER'S OFFER : £48,000

GAME 14

The correct answer was **DEAL.**
This was the highest offer The Banker made.

ROUND 05	BOX 19	BOX 18	BOX 3
AMOUNT	£1	£15,000	£75,000

BANKER'S OFFER : £1,700

ROUND 06	BOX 21	BOX 17	BOX 15
AMOUNT	£50	£750	£10,000

BANKER'S OFFER : £2,000

GAME 15

The correct answer was **NO DEAL.**
More money was to be won on ROUND 06.

ROUND 05	BOX 9	BOX 19	BOX 13
AMOUNT	1p	£10,000	£50,000

BANKER'S OFFER : £28,000

ROUND 06	BOX 10	BOX 17	BOX 14
AMOUNT	£5	£10	£3,000

BANKER'S OFFER : £59,000

ANSWERS

BEAT THE BANKER:
EXPERT

GAME 01

The correct answer was **NO DEAL.**
More money was to be won on ROUND 06.

ROUND 05	BOX 11	BOX 12	BOX 4
AMOUNT	10p	£10	£1,000

BANKER'S OFFER : £2,000

ROUND 06	BOX 13	BOX 22	BOX 14
AMOUNT	50p	£1	£50

BANKER'S OFFER : £13,000

GAME 02

The correct answer was **DEAL.**
This was the highest offer The Banker made.

ROUND 05	BOX 16	BOX 10	BOX 11
AMOUNT	1p	£500	£250,000

BANKER'S OFFER : £4,000

ROUND 06	BOX 17	BOX 3	BOX 21
AMOUNT	£1,000	£15,000	£35,000

BANKER'S OFFER : £400

GAME 03

The correct answer was **DEAL.**
This was the highest offer The Banker made.

ROUND 04	BOX 19	BOX 17	BOX 5
AMOUNT	50p	£500	£250,000

BANKER'S OFFER : £9,000

ROUND 05	BOX 7	BOX 10	BOX 8
AMOUNT	10p	£5	£100

BANKER'S OFFER : £18,200

ROUND 06	BOX 15	BOX 20	BOX 11
AMOUNT	£50	£35,000	£100,000

BANKER'S OFFER : £21,000

GAME 04

The correct answer was **NO DEAL.**
More money was to be won on ROUND 05.

ROUND 05	BOX 17	BOX 03	BOX 04
AMOUNT	1p	10p	£3,000

BANKER'S OFFER : £50,000

ROUND 06	BOX 18	BOX 14	BOX 19
AMOUNT	50p	£100	£500

BANKER'S OFFER : £16,000

GAME 05

The correct answer was **DEAL.**
This was the highest offer The Banker made.

ROUND 06	BOX 17	BOX 3	BOX 21
AMOUNT	£1,000	£15,000	£35,000

BANKER'S OFFER : £400

GAME 06

The correct answer was **DEAL.**
This was the highest offer The Banker made.

ROUND 05	BOX 21	BOX 18	BOX 11
AMOUNT	£10,000	£15,000	£75,000

BANKER'S OFFER : £3,000

ROUND 06	BOX 20	BOX 10	BOX 22
AMOUNT	£100	£1,000	£35,000

BANKER'S OFFER : £100

GAME 07

The correct answer was **NO DEAL.**
More money was to be won on ROUND 06.

ROUND 05	BOX 16	BOX 19	BOX 18
AMOUNT	10P	£100	£35,000

BANKER'S OFFER : £2,200

ROUND 06	BOX 20	BOX 15	BOX 17
AMOUNT	1p	£5,000	£10,000

BANKER'S OFFER : £5,000

GAME 08

The correct answer was **NO DEAL.**
More money was to be won on ROUND 06.

ROUND 05	BOX 18	BOX 10	BOX 19
AMOUNT	£5	£250	£3,000

BANKER'S OFFER : £17,000

ROUND 06	BOX 14	BOX 6	BOX 1
AMOUNT	1p	£750	£10,000

BANKER'S OFFER : £41,000

GAME 09

The correct answer was **NO DEAL.**
More money was to be won on ROUND 05.

ROUND 05	BOX 21	BOX 13	BOX 7
AMOUNT	1p	£750	£15,000

BANKER'S OFFER : £24,000

ROUND 06	BOX 6	BOX 4	BOX 14
AMOUNT	£500	£3,000	£250,000

BANKER'S OFFER : £4,000

GAME 10

The correct answer was **NO DEAL.**
More money was to be won on ROUND 06.

ROUND 05	BOX 5	BOX 3	BOX 14
AMOUNT	1p	£5	£50,000

BANKER'S OFFER : £8,000

ROUND 06	BOX 12	BOX 22	BOX 10
AMOUNT	£250	£500	£10,000

BANKER'S OFFER : £38,000

GAME 11

The correct answer was **DEAL.**
This was the highest offer The Banker made.

ROUND 06	BOX 11	BOX 4	BOX 5
AMOUNT	£250	£3,000	£250,000

BANKER'S OFFER : £37,000

GAME 12

The correct answer was **DEAL.**
This was the highest offer The Banker made.

ROUND 06	BOX 20	BOX 15	BOX 21
AMOUNT	10p	£10,000	£100,000

BANKER'S OFFER : £20

GAME 13

The correct answer was **DEAL.**
This was the highest offer The Banker made.

ROUND 06	BOX 12	BOX 14	BOX 17
AMOUNT	£100	£1,000	£250,000

BANKER'S OFFER : £1,400

GAME 14

The correct answer was **DEAL.**
This was the highest offer The Banker made.

ROUND 05	BOX 20	BOX 13	BOX 22
AMOUNT	£750	£20,000	£100,000

BANKER'S OFFER : £6,500

ROUND 06	BOX 1	BOX 17	BOX 2
AMOUNT	£10,000	£15,000	£50,000

BANKER'S OFFER : £2,100

GAME 15

The correct answer was **DEAL.**
This was the highest offer The Banker made.

ROUND 05	BOX 2	BOX 19	BOX 6
AMOUNT	£500	£3,000	£250,000

BANKER'S OFFER : £14,000

ROUND 06	BOX 8	BOX 18	BOX 22
AMOUNT	£1	£35,000	£75,000

BANKER'S OFFER : £400

GAME 16

The correct answer was **DEAL.**
This was the highest offer The Banker made.

ROUND 05	BOX 19	BOX 2	BOX 6
AMOUNT	50p	£100	£35,000

BANKER'S OFFER : £2,000

ROUND 06	BOX 4	BOX 12	BOX 22
AMOUNT	£1,000	£15,000	£20,000

BANKER'S OFFER : £200

AFTERWORD
BY THE BANKER

And so. Here we stand. You have taken on the might of the one and only Banker and you have lived to tell the tale. You can now rejoin your tiny life with a new sense of purpose. Congratulations, I salute you.

It's not easy, is it? I trust you have a new respect for all those poor, misguided souls who took me on for real, under the glare of the television lights. I hope you enjoyed the battle and that I haven't bruised you so very badly. But I did beat you, didn't I? Go on - admit it. I totally destroyed you. But don't feel downhearted. You were beaten by the best. I'm so very, very good at being very, very bad.

A few of you, a very few, may claim that you came out on top. You may crow that you defeated the mighty Banker and left him mewling like a pup.

Perhaps. But how did you manage it? How were you able you crush an intellectual Titan such as me?

I'll bet you looked at the answers.

So until the next time, my dear friend, I bid you a respectful goodbye. Perhaps we'll meet again in the pages of a future book. Perhaps we'll meet on the studio floor at Deal or No Deal. Or perhaps ...perhaps we'll meet tomorrow as you go about your business. Oh yes, that man in the shadows who just barely caught your eye...

That could be me.

Respectfully yours, chin, chin.

The Banker